THE PUBS OF
HASTINGS AND ST LEONARDS

1800–2000

◇————————◇

David Russell

Illustrated by James Gray

Published by Lynda Russell

Copies of this book are available from the publisher.
Email: hastings.pubs@gmail.com
Tel: 01424 200227

Printed by Athenaeum Press Limited, Gateshead

ISBN 978-0-9562917-0-7

Cover design by James Gray. Watercolours by Jean Hope.

Contents

Acknowledgements

To the excellent staff of Hastings Reference Library.

To members of the Pub History Society and Sussex CAMRA.

And in particular to: -

The late Charles Banks (and daughter Lucy) for wartime memories as a Hastings policeman.

Dr. Patrick Chaplin, pub and darts historian, for consulting his reference library and giving his time and expert opinion.

Jean Hope for her watercolours of the London Trader and the Marina Inn sign on the back cover and the assistance of The Old Gallery, George Street.

Trevor Hopper for checking the Robert Tressell connections.

Paul Jennings for references on the Shades.

Cyril Pelluet for research into the Jinks family.

Roger Povey of 'Arts For Arts Sake' for sharing his extensive knowledge of Hastings pub history with me over many communications.

Arthur R. Taylor for information on the 'Battle Shoot' and 'Four Corners' from his forthcoming book *'Played at the Pub'*.

Alan Crouch, Jim Davidson, Pat Dunn, Alan Garaty, Marie Garaty, Sergio Geurreiro, John Hodges, Trefor Holloway, Michael Monk, Mick Nurse, Cyril Pelluet, Roger Povey, Michael Rose and Peter Skinner for their pub memories.

My wife Lynda for designing and publishing this book, photographing the pubs, for her assistance with editing and finally for her company in visiting all the present-day pubs and sampling their wares.

Early drafts on the Warrior's Gate, Marina Fountain and the Anchor, East Ascent first appeared in the *Warrior* community newspaper 2007 – 8. A longer version of the 'Havelock' originally appeared in *'The Journal of the Pub History Society'*, 2007.

Introduction

It has been estimated that there were only fifteen public houses in Hastings in 1824, which at that time had a population of about 4,000. Obviously there were other drinking places, including unlicensed premises on America Ground* and elsewhere and a few beer houses.

Six years later the 1830 Beer Act saw the start of dozens of beer houses opening in the town, a trend which continued for the next forty years. In due course many of these became fully licensed public houses.

From 1828 the population grew rapidly with the building of St Leonards and the expansion of Hastings into the Priory Valley. Later, with the development of America Ground and the town centre from the 1850s, more public houses opened. By the 1870s the town was expanding outwards and new licences were granted in all districts of the town.

The high point of this expansion was 1860, when Hastings and St Leonards had a total of 128 pubs and beer houses, an average of one pub for every 110 people, which meant the town had one of the highest pub-population ratios in the country.

The Licensing Act of 1904 was the sting in the tail. This Act gave local magistrates the power to close down public houses on the grounds that they were redundant or no longer needed.

---

*An area of marshland created by a receding sea in the eighteenth century and inhabited by squatters until 1837.

From that year, the licensing magistrates applied the new law with indecent haste, encouraged by the chief constable and the local temperance lobby. The St Leonards branch of the British Women's Temperance Association cheered at its annual general meeting in 1905 as the closure of the first five pubs under this Act was announced.

However, twenty-three years later in 1928, Hastings still had one pub for every 328 people, which compared to Eastbourne, (1/574) or Blackpool (1/711), indicates that the town still had a very high pub-population ratio.

Forty years later, in 1945, according to the chief constable's own figures, eighty-nine pubs had been 'extinguished', although fifty-three new licences were granted in the same period. This brought the pub-population ratio down to about 1:450.

After the war, the policy of the Hastings magistrates was to transfer licences 'in suspension' to new pubs. Licences of war damaged pubs and others which had closed were transferred to new pubs mainly in the outlying districts of the town. Among others the Swan licence was transferred to the Wishing Tree, the Fortune of War licence to the New Broom in Malvern Way and the Denmark licence to the Comet in Harley Shute Road.

In 2006 Hastings had 368 licensed premises, although only 110 or so could accurately be described as pubs. Since research for this book began, several of these have closed. What follows is an historical account of some of the Hastings and St Leonards pubs, past and present. Some extant pubs have not been included for reasons of space. Recently the media have suggested that the pub is an outdated institution. All the more reason to record its history.

David Russell, St Leonards-on-Sea, May 2009

Admiral Benbow
London Road, St Leonards

The Admiral Benbow started life in 1833[1] and was the third public house to be built in the new town of St Leonards-on-Sea, being erected at that time by James Burton. It was first known as the Saxon Shades, a plebeian taproom at the rear of the Saxon Hotel (1832–1905). The hotel is now the Lotus Chinese restaurant on the corner of London Road.

Initially the hotel proprietor, William Eldridge, was refused a licence by the Hastings magistrates, who were under the influence of the Burton family. Burton claimed the Saxon hotel and Shades were outside the boundary of St Leonards, which in any case already had three other hotels. Eldridge, however, refused to accept this verdict and appealed to the magistrates at Lewes, who overturned the decision and granted the licence.[2]

The Hastings magistrates were cautious after this and over the next twenty-five years granted licences to at least fifteen public houses in central St Leonards. There were also several beer houses licensed by the Excise.

The Saxon Shades existed for half a century. It served the drivers and coachmen of the six-horse coaches that stopped there and the ostlers and stablemen who serviced them. The name 'shades' was a term used in the south-east for a tap room located behind a hotel, indicating that the premises were used by prostitutes (see page 194).

In 1884 the Saxon Shades changed its name to the Yorkshire Grey.[3] In 1898 the landlord was summonsed for allowing gambling on the premises, a story which hit the national headlines. The landlord, Lewis Hobbs, organised a Derby sweepstake on the run up to Derby day every year. This was run on the calculation that selling 1,000 tickets at 2s 6d [12½p], would generate a total of £125. Ten per cent was deducted for expenses and printing, leaving £112.10s [£112.50] for prizes. Tickets were sold openly over the bar. However, the police employed a man called Mawle, who formerly worked in the pub, to observe ticket sales and to note whether or not the gambling law was being broken. On Mawle's evidence the police raided the pub and the landlord was charged.

A jury convicted him at Lewes Assizes but he appealed. The case went to the Queen's Bench where, finally, five judges decided that the Yorkshire Grey sweepstake was a lottery that the landlord managed 'for the purpose of adding to the popularity of his house'. He received no profit and took no tickets. The prizewinners were decided, not on the outcome of the horse race itself, but on the drawing of the tickets. The conviction was quashed and Lewis Hobbs was exonerated. This case helped clarify what was and was not gambling in pubs all over the country.[4]

A century later the large upstairs room had become a popular 'pub rock' venue known as Blades. It was one of few live music venues in Hastings at the time and was organised by Phil Little, drummer with local group The Pullbacks.[5] Award-winning pianist and jazz singer Liane Carroll played there with the Trevor Francis Quartet, as did the Roger Carey Band and many others.

Trefor Holloway recalls: 'The pub I remember with affection is the Yorkshire Grey. It's closed now but in the eighties I worked sometimes in pub security. I worked as a bouncer on the door there. The Yorkshire "Gay" as it was dubbed was the most lively, popular and successful pub in the town.'[6]

The music stopped in 1995 when the pub closed temporarily after the landlady ran off with the takings and the jukebox. Soon after, it was renamed the Admiral Benbow, commemorating the seaman John Benbow (1650–1702), who died fighting the French in the Caribbean. His bravery is the subject of a folk ballad of the same name. Here are three verses of the East Sussex version: —

Oh, Benbow lost his legs, by chain-shot, by chain-shot,
Down on his stumps did fall and so loud for mercy called,
Oh fight on my British tars,
It is my lot, it is my lot.

Come all you seamen bold, landed here, landed here,
It is of an Admiral brave called Benbow by his name,
How he ploughed the raging main
You shall hear, you shall hear.

Last Tuesday morning last, Benbow died, Benbow died,
What a shocking sight to see when they carried him away
Oh, they carried him to Se'm's'on* church
There he lays, there he lays.[7]

The pub finally closed in 2008.

*Selmeston, East Sussex

Anchor Inn
East Ascent

The Anchor Inn opened in a yard behind East Ascent around 1833 and is one of the 'lost' pubs of St Leonards. The entrance to the yard and the pub was through a twitten,* then known as Anchor Passage. There was also a store and counting house in the yard, and a second passageway leading to coachmen's dwellings in St Leonards Mews. The mews has long disappeared and the yard is now a private back garden.

* Sussex term for a narrow passage or alleyway.

This beer house had an anchor above the door, a 'fouled anchor' with a rope curled round it. James Burton incorporated the sign of the anchor into the Burton family arms in 1902 and, at a later date, it became the coat of arms of St Leonards itself. Other versions of the St Leonards anchor can be seen on the Clock House, St Leonards Gardens, above the arch of North Lodge and on an old cast iron boundary marker.

In its early years the Anchor was not fully licensed and remained a simple beer house. This was due to James Burton promising Steven Milstead, landlord of the nearby Horse and Groom in Mercatoria, that there would be no fully licensed public house between the Horse and Groom and the St Leonards Hotel Tap (now the Royal Victoria Hotel). However, this agreement lasted only a few years.[1]

In the 1830s the bulk of the population was illiterate and newspapers were highly taxed to prevent poorer people having access to them. The Anchor, the Horse and Groom, the Tivoli Tavern and other local public houses had news rooms, where they employed 'Sunday readers' to recite the newspapers to the assembled customers. Amateur politicians of the day would gather to listen, discuss and criticise issues of local and national government.

A local schoolteacher was Sunday reader at the Anchor Inn for many years, a practice that stayed until the tax on newspapers was removed in 1855 and a Mechanics' Institute was established in St Leonards in the 1850s.

These were exciting years and, although it might not seem much to us now, one of the major issues up for discussion was the 1832 Reform Act, which gave the vote to men who owned or leased land worth £10 or more. This was the start of popular suffrage and the right to vote, which was celebrated by thousands of people in Hastings with bonfires on the beach and overflowing pubs. For many years after 1832 the Anchor celebrated the anniversary of the Reform Act on 'the glorious first of June'.

One landlord in the 1850s was under the impression that he could serve his friends when he wished. On more than one occasion drinkers, cautioned by the police after hours, claimed they were only there as friends of the landlord. During one case the clerk of the court asked a customer: 'How do you address your friends in the Anchor?' 'Good morning. I want a pint of Porter.' [laughter]

In 1869, landlord Thomas Vido was fined for allowing gambling on the premises. Ostlers who worked in the stables in Mews Road looking after the horses for the coaches of the nearby St Leonards Hotel, were among the customers who played cards for money. This sometimes got out of hand and led to cheating and argument.

In its final years the Anchor was tied to the Blyth Brewery (later Ind Coope) for draught beer, but was a free house for bottles and spirits. Tom Wells was landlord for twenty-five years but, it was said, he died penniless, totally impoverished and destitute.[2] The Anchor started to lose trade around 1900 and the police complained it was difficult to supervise the pub through the twitten. From 1900 it had at least five different landlords before being forced to close by the licensing magistrates in 1905, using their new powers under the Act of 1904.

Along with four other lost pubs, the Hastings Castle, the Eagle Tavern, the Warrior's Arms and the Free Trader, the Anchor was one of the first pubs in Hastings to be declared redundant. The landlord was compensated with a handsome payment of £800.[3] In today's terms, according to the historic retail price index, this would be equivalent to around £59,000.

Anchor Inn
George Street, Old Town

Another Anchor Inn dated back to at least 1680 and stood outside the Old Town wall, near the fish market. The current Anchor Inn, George Street, dates back to 1798, when the licensee was Anne Thwaites.[1] This was an era when the population was largely illiterate and when pubs were recognised by visual symbols and signs, instead of written names. Hence the small anchor embedded in the wall above the door. The sign of the Anchor was a popular one for pubs near the sea.

For over two centuries the Anchor has had a wide variety of customers. In the early 1800s, military personnel were billeted in the Anchor and in the surrounding streets, in anticipation of an invasion by Napoleon. Later in the century, auctioneers used the pub to auction local property. Before the advent of the welfare state, it was the headquarters of a large branch of Oddfellows and was also one of Hastings's fishing pubs with, at one time, a 5am licence for fishermen, fish buyers and hawkers at the fish market. And of course, it has always been popular with summer visitors.

From 1805 to 1840 the landlord was Thomas Daniels.[2]

> Tom Daniels lives here, a most worthy old chum,
> Who sells the best brandy, gin, hollands and rum—
> He caters for tradesmen and sailors alot,
> And serves up for farmers, good dinners all hot;
> With nimblest of feet and the strongest of nerves
> It's said that his patrons be very well served
> From widow Anne Thwaites he the Anchor obtained,
> In 1805 he the licence first gained.

From 1840 to the late 1860s, the landlord was Charles West, who kept a respected and well-run public house, accommodating large numbers of customers for Oddfellows, Friendly Society meetings and dinners, in the Assembly Room, leased by West next door.[3]

From 1753 to 1833, the Assembly Room was a pub called the Rose and Crown. In 1833 it was replaced by a new fish market resented by the fishing community who wanted to continue selling fish on the beach. The market later became the Assembly Room. Today it is known as the Black Market.

As the centre of Hastings moved from the Old Town to the Priory Valley, Charles West went with the flow and moved into Robertson Street in 1868, where he took over the premises now known as The Street, but then known as West's Cellars. One of his last acts before leaving was to raise money for new bells for St Clement's Church.[4]

With the departure of Charles West, the Anchor slid downhill into a murky period of its history. Local prostitutes were allowed to ply their trade, thieves and pickpockets were among the customers and the pub was always in the news for drunkenness, gambling, riotous and immoral behaviour. Not surprisingly it was often threatened with closure, but has somehow managed to survive.

ANCHOR INN
OLD TOWN HASTINGS

ON DRAUGHT

FERDINANDS FOLLY

A full-bodied Dry Red Wine
1/9 per large glass
5/6 per bottle   Off sales

LUNCHES SERVED
12 – 2.30

In a typical incident in 1871, a prostitute called Harriet Clapson, was charged with assaulting a woman from London. The London woman came into the 'little room' of the pub and Clapson remarked that she would 'show these ... from London who come down here and do the bounce on us'. She delivered a violent blow with her fist to the woman's head, for which she was fined 10s [50p] plus 9s.6d costs.[5]

Five years later, one of the most serious riots in the history of the town broke out at the Anchor. A drunk refused to leave when asked, and assaulted the landlord. He was arrested and a riotous crowd assembled. Stones were thrown at the police in response to the man's incitement of the crowd to rescue him. 'This is a good chance to hustle the police', he shouted and a large, violent crowd did just that. More stones were thrown, one seriously denting the constable's helmet. In response, the constable had to call for assistance and it finally took four constables to overpower the man and take him away. A violent mob followed them to the station house and remained outside for some time until they were cleared. In Hastings Borough Court the man was found guilty of assaulting the landlord, refusing to quit the pub and incitement to riot. He was sent to Lewes prison for a period of hard labour.[6]

The police station was one of the few civic buildings to remain in the Old Town where it was needed, in the late Victorian period.

Since the 1950s, the Anchor has had to compete with the Pump House opposite. Remembering the Anchor from that time, Cyril Pelluet recalled: 'Sometimes we went across the road to the Anchor where they served draught scrumpy and draught Cypress wine by the glass.'[7] Another draught wine sold there was Ferdinand's Folly, a dry red, at 1s 9d [9p] a large glass. This was in 1959.

Michael Rose thought the Anchor public bar was rather rough in the 1960s,[8] but by the 1980s things had changed. Pat Dunn used the saloon, which was a bit of a 'yuppy bar', and remembers the traditional jazz bands that played there.[9]

The back bar of the Anchor was at one time used as a courtroom, where local criminals were tried and sentenced for various crimes. This could explain why the ghost of a judge in a dark suit and black hat haunts the back bar, making sure that today's customers are behaving. Thus the Anchor covets the title of 'most haunted pub' in Hastings and the Old Town Ghost walks start from here in the summer.

Angel and the Plough
West Hill

These two pubs on the West Hill both opened as beer houses in 1835.[1] The Angel, first known as the Brisco Arms, took its name from the Brisco family who resided at Bohemia House. Musgrave Brisco was the conservative member of parliament for Hastings in 1844. The name changed to the Angel in 1837, when Henry Morley, formerly a tailor, became the landlord. He was also a journalist and a liberal and probably changed the pub name for political reasons.

At that time the Angel stood in the Long Field, now called St Mary's Terrace, while the Plough stood in the Mill Field, so called because there was a cluster of four windmills on the West Hill, with another further away on the site of the present priory schools. One windmill was situated in the garden of the Plough, and the last survived until 1874.

In the 1840s, the landlord of the Plough worked as a wheelwright, running the beer house as a secondary occupation.[2] The Plough got a full licence in 1854 but in 1856 the landlady, Martha Rhoden, became bankrupt and was unable to pay the General District Rate of 18s [90p]. She had to move out and apply for a 'distress warrant'.

Both inns must have had the custom of the millers, carters and other workers in the corn trade, as well as those who worked in the local slaughterhouses in the area. As the West Hill area was developed in the last thirty years of the nineteenth century and the first houses were completed, itinerant building workers and travelling tradesmen were customers of both pubs. Some used the Angel as a lodging house.[3]

The Angel stands over St Clement's Caves, which cover a large area under the West Hill. It is thought that the Angel used the caves as a pub cellar for several years, although the management of St Clement's Caves cannot confirm this.

The American artist, James McNeil Whistler (1834–1903), probably used both pubs when visiting his mother at nearby Talbot House, St Mary's Terrace. Over a period of six years he painted her portrait, which now hangs in the Louvre in Paris. Nearby, Whistler's Steps lead down into the Priory Valley and the town centre.

In 1871 the Angel landlord, John Crouch, was summonsed and fined 'for having his house open during the hours of divine service on Good Friday'.[4] Some years later another landlord, Harry Johnson, spent a lot of time as a soapbox orator, debating with socialists in the cut and thrust of local Edwardian politics.

In his younger days, Johnson had been an Independent Labour Party speaker, but changed his politics in later life. In a debate with the Hastings firebrand Alf Cobb, Johnson became irritated by a remark about the iniquities of brewers and publicans. He was also upset by jibes about 'publicans, beer and angels'. 'What about strawberries?' his supporters replied. (Cobb was a barrow boy later summoned for obstructing the roadway, whilst selling strawberries outside the Old England.)[5]

During the First World War, the Angel was closed from May 1916, when the landlord was called up into the military. He didn't return and the pub stayed closed until December 1920. This led the licensing magistrates to conclude that the pub was redundant and in 1921 it was referred to the compensation authority for closure, along with the Little Brown Jug, a beer house 'forty-five paces away' in St Mary's Terrace.

In 1921 several surprise visits were made by the police to pubs in the area, to establish their custom. In nine visits they found a total of '121 customers in the Angel, 264 in the Granville, 136 in the Whitefriars, 128 in the Plough, but only forty-seven in the Little Brown Jug'. The more middle class Red House was ignored by the police and left alone.[6] The Angel and the Plough were both opposed by the temperance lobby, in this case the Sunday School Union and the British Women's Temperance Association, but finally the magistrates decided to close the Little Brown Jug and not the Angel, as there was not enough money to compensate both.

The Angel came to attention in 1977, when eighteen-year-old Mark Greenaway of the Angel darts team got within one second of the world record for 'round the board doubles at arm's length'. The landlord of the Warrior's Gate in St Leonards, held the world record of 9.2 seconds.[7]

Years before the smoking ban in public buildings, the Angel supported National No Smoking Day campaigns. As early as 1988, along with the local Health Promotion Unit, the landlord designated the ground floor of the pub as a 'No Smoking' area. He said the smoke free area was being promoted to encourage people to give up smoking and to reduce the incidence of passive smoking. Although the campaign didn't have total national support, one and a half million people attempted to give up smoking. It is not known how many succeeded. The Angel was the only pub in Hastings known to participate in the national 'No Smoking' campaign at that time. The Angel finally closed in the economic recession of 2008.

The Plough is a building of Dutch design which maybe connected with the windmill that once stood in its garden. Its sign depicts the plough constellation.

Barrattinis's Sports Bar
Marina, St Leonards

James Burton built the Marina in 1829, as part of the new town of St Leonards-on-Sea. For 146 years, 42 Marina was the home of Addison's, the town's oldest established bakers and confectioners.[1] Addison's advertised itself as 'a connoisseur of exotic food', supplying the upper class market of Victorian St Leonards and in later years the large American export market, until the last member of the family, K. E. Addison, retired.

In 1975 the property was sold and became Mr Cherry's Wine Bar, which was opened by TV star, David Lloyd Meredith, of *Softly, Softly* fame.[2] It got off to a good start, supported by the Hastings branch of the Campaign for Real Ale, which had been formed in the Prince Albert, Brook Street. CAMRA used Mr Cherry's for branch meetings[3] and the pub quickly became established for its real ale and as one of the town's best known 'pub rock' venues. In 1976 it celebrated its first birthday with optimism and was listed in the *CAMRA Good Beer Guide.*

In 1983 a micro-brewery was installed in the basement, the home of Addison's original bakery, and started brewing Conqueror Bitter.[4] Because of its strength (it had a gravity of 10.66) it was sold only in half pints. This was the first micro-brewery in Hastings in modern times, three years before the FILO brewery opened in 1986, although the FILO brewery is still operating. Subsequently, Mr Cherry's was listed in the *Good Beer Guide* from 1983 to 1986.

Mr Cherry's logo

In 1983 the Hastings Jack in the Green festival was revived on May Day, after an absence of three quarters of a century. The route of the procession in the first few years visited St Leonards Gardens, behind Mr Cherry's, (where the original nineteenth century Jack in the Green celebrations took place) and refreshment was taken in Mr Cherry's by revellers dressed as trees, before they marched back to the Stade.

In 1988 the magistrates refused to renew Mr Cherry's music licence due to complaints about noise. A few weeks after this decision, the pub suddenly closed and reopened as the James Burton, with the promise of strict noise control, for the benefit of the middle aged and elderly residents in the area.[5]

After a steady start and a new music licence, the James Burton spiralled into a tumultuous existence, with a continuous conflict between the licensees, the Marine Court Residents Association, the licensing magistrates and Hastings Borough Council. It acquired the nickname of 'the hash joint' and there were continuous complaints of a 'hooligan element, injuries to off-duty police, noise, loud music, a riff-raff occupying the front pavement, drugs, motor bikes and general mayhem in the evenings'.[6] It seems however, that these complaints were only half accurate and exaggerated.

From 1975 until 1990 many popular bands and musicians from Hastings and elsewhere played here. Roger Carey's Upstarts, Buick 6 and Pass the Cat, three popular Hastings groups, performed here, as did the Liane Carroll Big Band and the eighteen-piece Sounds of Swing. Among the musicians from outside the town were Howlin Wilf and the Vee-Jays, known for their album *Blue Men Sing the Whites*.

Once more the renewal of the music licence was refused and six months after the closure of Mr Cherry's the James Burton was served with a Noise Abatement Notice, but the music continued. Eventually the two joint licensees were each fined £2,000 plus £2,500 costs, although they had spent £8,000 insulating the proposed Burtoneon Club in the basement. In 1990, after a heady two years, the pub suddenly closed for a second time.[7]

The closure was of concern to the Hastings pub rock community and, with fewer venues available to them, they started to organise. In 1993 the Hastings Live Music Forum was set up. It was chaired by Phil Little, drummer with the Pullbacks, and began to lobby for more venues. In 1994 another pub music venue, the Carlisle, which had been threatened with closure, was reprieved. A second pub music venue, Pissarro's, opened at the same time. Ironically Phil Little moved to Canada.

The local press reported the James Burton as 'Gone For a Burton' and with the licensees bankrupt, the business went into receivership. In 1994 it was put up for sale, but it was not until 2003 that it reopened as Kollege Kantina, which ran for four years and was popular with students of the college in Archery Road. Kollege Kantina closed in 2007 and reopened in 2008 as Burton's Bar. In 2009 it had another name change to Barrattinis's Sports Bar.

Bo Peep
Grosvenor Crescent, St Leonards

The Bo Peep is linked with the coming of the railways to Hastings, with smugglers and with a well-known nursery rhyme. Over its lifetime it has had four name changes and has been rebuilt at least once. The original pub, known as the New England Bank Inn, was apparently shown on a map of 1746.[1] By the time of the Napoleonic Wars, it took the name Bo Peep after the name of a Martello Tower or small fort, across the road. It drew its custom from the many active smugglers in these parts and from the two hundred soldiers billeted nearby.

New England Bank

The Hastings Guide, published in 1794 by James Barry, described the Bo Peep as 'a public house by the roadside, where company may have an excellent dish of tea and good cream al fresco'.[2] The pub is mentioned again in 1815 as 'a wretched public house by the roadside', although this didn't deter the poet John Keats and the beautiful Isabella Jones from staying there when he visited the south coast in 1817. Keats portrayed Isabella Jones, 'the lady from Hastings', in his poem Endymion,[3] a poetic romance published in 1818 depicting a nymph rising naked from the Fishponds, a local Bulverhythe beauty spot. The poem is famous for its first line: *A thing of beauty is a joy forever*.

When the railway arrived along the coast from Brighton in 1846, the original pub was demolished to make way for West Marina station (where Carpetright now stands).

Where sailors, soldiers, smugglers all
Hob nobbed in days of yore;
That wayside inn whose site just now
The railway covers o'er.[4]

By all accounts riotous times were had in the old pub. A musician who played there in the 1840s observed that the 'dancing created abnormal vibration. The visible contraction of the old walls was such as to threaten a general collapse!'[5]

The landlord was compensated by the South Eastern Railway Company and in 1847 he built a new pub, just east of the new station.[6] The new pub was at first called the Railway Terminus Inn and supplied beer to passengers waiting for the coach into Hastings. The name reverted back to Bo Peep when the tunnel was dug through the cliffs behind, and the railway line continued into St Leonards. In 1972 when the site of the New England Bank was excavated and developed, old wine bottles, a silver fork and a mineral bottle dated 1808 were found.

In the mid-Victorian era the Bo Peep was a popular venue. Apart from political meetings, balls, quadrilles and parties were held here on a regular basis. It was a meeting place for the St Leonards vestry, who discussed parish matters and elected the local rate collector.

In 1843 two overseers
Not one of whom in flesh now appears
A rate prescribed at that New England Bank
Which bounded St Leonards western flank.
That wayside Inn, near where grazing sheep,
Made way for railway station at Bo Peep.

As a 'railway pub', coroner's inquests into accidents on the line took place here. A moment of tragedy came in 1877, with the death of a guard on a train travelling through Bo Peep tunnel. He must have been looking out of the window when a train passing in the opposite direction struck him dead. Nobody saw anything as the tunnel was full of steam.[7] There was a second accident a few years later, when a body and severed head were found on the line by a signalman, who took them to the stables at the rear of the pub. Both accidents were severe shocks to the local community.

In 1962 the Bo Peep was one of the first local pubs to hold a wine tasting event, an interest that slowly developed after the war. A large number of customers turned up to try the sherry, port, Bordeaux, Burgundy, Portuguese and German wines.

Academics and others have tried to explain the connection between Bo Peep and smuggling. In fact Bo Peep the nursery rhyme is a metaphor. Its exact origin is uncertain, but locals claim it as an old St Leonards tale and there is no doubt that the pub was used by smugglers, as shown on one side of the pub sign. The other side shows a shepherdess. The Bo Peep double sign was unveiled in 1977.

The metaphor of Bo Peep refers to the customs men (looking and peeping), the sheep refers to the smugglers (who they cannot find) and their tails to the contraband (barrels of rum and brandy).

The headquarters of the Hastings pipe band, 1066 Pipes and Drums, is nearby. They play locally but have also played at Menim Gate in Belgium and in New York. They are a colourful addition to the Bo Peep custom after band practice.

Bulverhythe
Bexhill Road

Although over 150 years old, there is more history in the location of this pub, in its name, and its sign, than in the building itself. The pub is located in the old Cinque Port 'lymbe' of Bulverhythe, one of the 'lost villages' of Sussex.

The old English name hythe simply means 'people's landing place'. Although Pevensey is the officially recognised landing place for William the Conqueror, the precise spot where he landed is still a debating point among a minority of historians, some of whom claim that Bulverhythe, as the port of old Hastings, is a possible landing place.

The pub sign has nothing to do with William the Conqueror or the Cinque Ports, but shows a ship that was wrecked off the Bulverhythe coast in a severe gale in 1749. The ship in question was a Dutch East Indiaman called the *Amsterdam* and the pub sign is a copy of a painting of it, commissioned by the *Holland Herald*, an English language Dutch newspaper and painted by Jean Moore of St Leonards in 1975.

The *Amsterdam*, on her maiden voyage from North Holland to Indonesia, encountered a severe storm in the North Sea and lost her rudder. She attempted to anchor but drifted ashore at Bulverhythe where she sank into the beach mud.

At night at low tide, the crew clambered down the sides of the ship and were taken to safety by the locals. Smugglers quickly raided the ship and removed a large number of silver coins from the hold. After the rest of the bullion was officially removed, the town crier tried to locate and recover the missing silver, but without much success.

The wreck sank further into the soft beach mud and the remains of three decks are still buried, with much of her cargo and supplies, including onion-shaped bottles of Monbazillac, a French wine, intact. In 1969 an attempt was made to salvage the remains of the cargo and during the dig, some of the wine, vases and a cannon ball were looted.

The Bulverhythe is listed in the *Sussex Directory* for 1855[1] and was probably a beer house from about 1850, serving the railway navvies building the line into Hastings, and stage coach travellers on the Bexhill Road.

In 1900, along with some other local pubs and shops, the Bulverhythe became a victim of a nineteenth century confidence trick known as the 'bright farthing'. The barmaid had to constantly watch out for customers who paid for their beer with a sovereign [£1], which meant that there would usually be a half sovereign in the change. A half sovereign was similar in size to a (polished) farthing, [a quarter of penny] which could, by sleight of hand, be substituted for the half sovereign and the change queried. This happened several times before the culprit was finally caught.[2]

Because of its location about three miles from the centre of Hastings, the Bulverhythe was also targeted by 'bona fide travellers', a new category of customer, created by the licensing laws of 1855 and 1872. These Acts introduced restrictions on pub opening hours, but gave travellers the right to be served in pubs outside of the usual hours. In 1910 two men from Hastings knocked on the door at 11.15 on a Sunday morning, asking to be served as travellers. At that time opening hours were from noon on a Sunday, but this did not apply to customers who had travelled at least three miles from where they had spent the previous night. They were observed by a policeman and charged.

In court they claimed they had travelled three miles. There was some dispute as to the distance from Hastings to Bulverhythe. The case was adjourned whilst the magistrates did some measuring. They decided that the distance from Hastings was two hundred yards [183m] short of the required three miles, but when the men were re-summonsed, the case was dismissed. Thus, before the First World War, the Bulverhythe quickly developed a reputation as, a pub where Hastingers could claim to be 'bona fide travellers' and get a drink outside normal pub hours.[3]

In the 1980s the Bulverhythe was a popular off-duty rendezvous for members of the Hastings police force, many of whom resided in the police flats in Harley Shute Road. It is now popular with residents and visitors staying at Combe Haven Holiday Park opposite.[4]

THE
BULVERHYTHE

Carlisle
Carlisle Parade

The Carlisle, formerly the Pelham Arms, was built by Richard Chandler in about 1820[1] on the site of an old tannery. It was located next door to a boat hull on America Ground, known as Noah's Ark. The Pelham Arms remained in the Chandler family until 1864 and was a meeting place for early rowing clubs and licensed watermen. Live music was played here in the 1840s[2] and by the 1880s it was known as a Liberal house.

In 1892 the Pelham Arms became the Carlisle Hotel.[3] The landlord, T.C. Brown, was a county cricketer and straw hat manufacturer. On the road to bankruptcy, he ignored all the signs and continued to take money out of the till, played cricket for Sussex 'a few times' and gambled a little on the side. By 1894 he had become bankrupt.[4]

Nineteenth century

In 1899 the pub was taken over by E.E. Chase, whose time here was to be even shorter than Brown's and he too became bankrupt within eighteen months. A reckless, extravagant character, Chase founded the Carlisle Cup, which was presented annually to local footballers.[5] When the Cinque Ports Volunteers went to the Boer War in 1900, he sent them boxes of expensive cigars.

One morning in 1908 a military impostor walked in pretending to be deaf and dumb. He produced a begging letter addressed to himself as a band sergeant from an army captain and was given a shilling [5p]. He got away with it until someone suddenly asked him if he would like a drink. 'A small Bass', he replied, and got three months for deception!

During the First World War, when the town was taken over by the military, a soldier from the South Wales Borderers sold his boots to a fruit hawker in the bar for 4s 4d [21½p], two oranges and a pot of beer. He was punished by his regiment and the hawker was fined. The licensee was then Harry Bishop, who at various times ran the Rising Sun, the King's Head and the Lord Nelson. He was called up into the army in 1917 and his wife took over.

During the inter-war years, the pub grew in success. By 1933 it had a popular roof terrace[6] and in the late 1930s it was extensively refurbished, with a dance floor and lounge for large-scale social occasions and became a major venue for some of the town's annual billiards, snooker and darts tournaments. In 1938 it staged the first ladies' snooker match to be played in public in Hastings, between N. Lawrence and T. Kirkpatrick.[7]

The Carlisle closed in the Second World War until May 1945 when it was one of only two local pubs with a music licence.[8] The Debonairs Dance Band played here twice a week and by the 1950s Carlisle Parade, then known as Teddy Boys' Walk, was the scene of clashes between 'Teds' and soldiers from Lydd Army Camp.

One popular Ted known as the Lemon Drop Kid used to sing Buddy Holly numbers and the pub hosted a Teddy Girl disc jockey called Bebopa Lula.

By the 1960s the lounge had become the Ocean Bar, hosting the Commanders Show Band. From then it attracted different youth cultures. After the Teds came the Rockers and in the 1980s the Greasers and Hell's Angels. By the 1980s the Carlisle had become a haunt of bikers from all over the country. In 1989 the leader of a Birmingham motor cycle gang was shot dead outside the pub by a member of the rival London Road Rats, who was jailed for life. Local band Die Laughing had to cancel their gigs during the following weeks.[9]

In 1992 Hastings Borough Council, who held the freehold threatened to close the pub down. A campaign was launched in its support and 12,000 people signed a petition. At one point 'thought waves' were sent out by the high priest and priestess of British white witches, Kevin and Ingrid Carlyon, in an attempt to cleanse the mind of the town council and persuade it to leave the Carlisle alone.[10] It was proposed to burn an old motor bike with an effigy of the council leader, below the high tide mark on the beach. At a crowded council meeting, Gus Cummins, a local artist, said that 'the Carlisle was unique to the town and had a colourful and diverse clientele'. Finally in 1994, the council decided the pub would stay open.

Every May Day thousands of bikers ride into town on the Hastings Run' and the Carlisle is at the hub of the day's activity. The Jack in the Green parade also takes place on May Day and these two large groups mix in their thousands. Bikers and on lookers get their noses daubed green and everyone has a good time.

There is some irony in the fact, that the pub is named after the crown agent who evicted the original inhabitants of America Ground in 1835, when today's customers are the true inheritors of the spirit of those times.

The high priest and priestess of British white witches

Cinque Ports Arms
All Saints Street, Old Town

The Cinque Ports Arms is one of Hastings's oldest pubs. It was formerly known as the Chequers, which apparently existed on this site in 1642, although the building has not been open continuously as a pub since that time.[1] It has been claimed that the current building replaced the original one several years ago. What is known is that the present building was partly rebuilt in the mock tudor style after a fire in 1925, and that the cottage next door was also 'tudorised' after the Second World War.

The fortunes of the Cinque Ports Arms have ebbed and flowed across the centuries, following the changing social fabric of the Old Town itself. In the seventeenth century it was described as a 'tenement block' with a dubious status, attached to an equally dubious brewery. The first mention of it as the Cinque Ports Arms was in 1827, when William Wood purchased the pub for £260. It is recorded that smugglers used the pub as a rendezvous and for storing contraband.[2]

From about 1850 the middle classes began to leave the Old Town and many of the public houses, if they were to stay open, had to accommodate the custom of tramps, hawkers, fish sellers and labourers. A common practice for those without money was to offer goods for drink. In the 1870s a tramp tried to exchange a slop (a loose outer garment or smock) for beer. He asked the landlord to let him have 'three pots on it', but was refused and went outside and sold it for 1s [5p] in the street.[3] During these years of poverty, the pub couldn't shake off its rough image. An attempt was made to auction it off at the start of the last century, but there were few bids. It didn't even make the reserve price and was withdrawn. Soon after, the chief constable tried to close the pub down, on the basis that it was just a common lodging house with a bar attached. The landlord quickly made some alterations to prevent communication between the lodging house and the pub, by separating the two. The Cinque Ports Arms was reprieved, but only just.

By 1905 it was still feeling the pinch of poverty. The pub was now only open part time and the landlord was forced to work as a hawker during the daytime. In 1919 there was a further attempt to close it down, this time because the chief constable considered the pub to be 'ill conducted' and, he said, because it was still attracting an undesirable custom. But again it was reprieved.

In recent decades the middle classes have moved back into the area and land values have dramatically increased. Ironically because of this, the Cinque Ports Arms was again threatened with closure in 1989. This time not because of poverty, but because the brewery, with an eye on the building as a valuable and desirable residence, considered turning it into a normal house. However, some think the brewery may have been opposed to the fact that the pub was generally seen as a gay pub. Fortunately this didn't happen.[4]

The Old Town, now one of the more affluent areas of Hastings, has found new fortunes and the Cinque Ports Arms has benefited from an improved local economy and from tourism. It is probably the only Hastings pub where the landlord calls time on a brass bell and, true to its age, a dark medieval atmosphere pervades its single bar.

The Cinque Ports of Hastings, Hythe, Romney, Dover and Sandwich have had their own coat of arms for many hundreds of years. Early common seals suggest that the design of three lions 'passant guardant' (full face), with one paw raised, conjoined to three ships' hulls, came into use between 1194 and 1305. The arms are derived from the golden lions used on the arms of England, except that the lions are joined with ships' hulls, to denote the provision of ships and men by the Cinque Ports to the Crown, before England had a navy.

The arms of the town of Hastings, on the other hand, differ in that they have only two lions conjoined to ships' hulls. The third lion is complete, which denotes Hastings as the chief Cinque Port.

41

Clarence
Middle Street

The Clarence, Middle Street, was built and licensed in 1868 as a small, town centre hotel.[1] Since then it has served a wide variety of customers, including army volunteers, building workers, trade unionists, benefit societies, football supporters and many others.

The 1st Cinque Ports Rifle Volunteer Corps, formed in 1860 and supported by public subscription, had its drill hall two doors away. Military personnel of all ranks were customers of the Clarence, who in the 1880s used the pub to host naval artillery suppers.[2] A second pub, the Volunteer, now gone, was located at the other end of Middle Street.

Before the mass production of cigarettes at the end of the nineteenth century, clay pipes were commonly smoked in pubs and it was the custom for the landlord to supply them free. The Clarence kept a jar of clay pipes on the bar. When a customer had finished his smoke he replaced the pipe in the jar for the next customer. Squeamish customers would break off an inch of stem to get a clean smoke. It was also the custom for the landlord to leave clay pipes in a cast iron rack over the fire at night, to sterilise them for the following day's patrons.[3]

The nineteenth century town centre was always busy with hawkers and on one occasion in 1872, a peddler walked in selling clay pipes. He had seventy for sale, for which he wanted 9d [4p]. 'Here's a little lot that will suit you Sir', he said to the landlord. When challenged by a constable he admitted he didn't have a hawker's licence, 'only one or two marriage certificates at home' [laughter].[4]

The period from the 1890s to the First World War was the heyday of the Clarence. These were very busy years. The Hastings Cabmen's Benefit Society held monthly meetings here. Their 'distress fund' was organised for the relief of members fallen on hard times. On one occasion a donation was made to a member whose trap had been smashed in the town centre. The cabmen also spent many evenings in 'harmony' (singing).[5]

The Clarence was also the meeting place of the Amalgamated Society of House Decorators and Painters, who ran an impressive campaign on wages and on the levelling up of the painter's rate to 7d [3p] an hour.[6] This determined the income of one drinker, Robert Tressell, who became the pub's most famous customer.

The Hastings branch of the Postmen's Federation, originally formed at the Clifton, St Leonards in 1895, also met here. The Hastings branch of the Amalgamated Society of Tailors, defunct in the 1890s, reformed here in 1906.[7] It was perhaps inevitable that the Hastings and St Leonards Trades Council was founded here in 1894.

Following this, the Hastings Labour Party, then known as the Labour Representation Committee, was formed by the Trades Council and the National Democratic League at the turn of the last century. It was here that debates about municipal housing, direct labour, public baths, fair wages, local hospital provision and other issues were debated, before being passed on to Hastings Borough Council and other authorities. It was from this pub that the Trades Council lobbied the candidates in national and local elections and then decided whom to support, on the basis of their replies.

By the time of the 1906 general election, the local trades union vote was significant enough for local candidates to canvas the votes of Trades Council members. This resulted in the Trades Council supporting the Liberal. Nevertheless, although twenty-nine Labour MPs were elected nationally and led by Keir Hardie, Hastings returned yet another Tory MP. In fact Hastings and Rye were the only two Conservative gains in the country.

In the same year the Hastings Labour Representation Committee split into two, when the trades unionists refused to break their links with the Liberals and Conservatives.[8] The Hastings and St Leonards Trades Council was still meeting here in 1951.

The Clarence has also been patronised by many other organisations over the years. These include Hastings Rowing Club, the Cinque Ports Foresters (a large branch with hundreds of members), the Victoria Lodge of the Oddfellows and the Hastings branch of the Equitable Society. The latter met here from 1901 and in 1910 the landlord formed the Clarence Benefit Society, which had 176 members and a total fund of £1,276, a considerable balance for those days. Between them, the members of all the above organisations provided the Clarence with a wide customer base.

During the Second World War the Clarence was patronised by Canadian troops billeted in the town. The late Charles Banks, then Police Inspector Banks, recalled that 'Hastings police were frequently called to the Clarence to deal with assaults, brawls and wilful damage. The ringleaders were frequently Canadian soldiers, members of the Princess Louise Dragoon Guards.'[9] During the war much of Middle Street was bombed, but the Clarence was spared.

Clarence@Silverhill
London Road, Silverhill

Originally trading in 1869 as a wine and spirit merchant, the Clarence@Silverhill became a public house in 1871. A small branch of the Oddfellows, the Clarence Lodge, with only thirty-five members, was formed here in 1872.

In 1873 a young domestic servant girl who lived nearby fell pregnant without realising it. She went into labour assuming she was ill and went to bed. In the final stage of labour she screamed out in agony. Her mother raced upstairs to find a stillborn baby on the floor. A coroner's inquest was held in the Clarence saloon into the death of the baby and two doctors established that the cause of death was strangulation by umbilical cord.[1]

A summons in 1889 revealed some extravagant drinking habits. The drunk and disorderly behaviour of five customers was blamed on a young landlord, criticised for a lack of experience. Barmaid Beatrice Elphick, who gave evidence in court, said: 'Six people drank seven bottles of champagne and ale, paid for by a traveller'. The outcome was that landlord Charles Goldsmith had his licence revoked.[2] This incident marked the beginning of a bad period for the Clarence.

In 1905 the first tram to Silverhill ended its journey at the tram depot, behind the Clarence in Beaufort Road. The Clarence Hotel then became a recognised stop on the route.

First tram to Silverhill, 1905

From 1890 until the First World War, the Clarence went through an unstable period, with nine different landlords and several incidents of drunkenness and rowdy behaviour. Referred to as the Silverhill Riots, a typical incident at the end of one evening in 1913 developed when an unruly mob of at least 100 people gathered outside and created a riotous disturbance. The police had a hard time dispersing the crowd and the landlord was heavily fined for allowing 'drunkenness, fighting and disorder'.[3]

The following year he was convicted a second time for serving two men at 2.30am. He claimed they were 'potmen' moving casks and cleaning the beer engine. In his defence, he said he had been a first-class petty officer in the navy and that he was a Freeman of the City of London and had 'frozen the tap' (i.e. barred) some of his more unruly customers. One customer, who claimed he was 'working' in the pub was asked: 'Did you restock the bar?' 'I had one or two', he said [laughter].[4]

In 1915 the chief constable opposed the renewal of the pub's licence, on the grounds that it was a den of 'thieves, poachers, men convicted of assaulting the police and other persons of bad character'. However, the magistrates noted that the licence had been transferred to a new landlord (again), that the late licensee William McGinty had moved on and that there was some improvement. Consequently, the Clarence stayed open.

The licence was probably transferred because, during the First World War, all publicans were expected to be British subjects and McGinty, although technically a British subject, was Irish.[5]

In the middle of the war Henry Burnett took over and remained landlord for thirty years, creating the stability the Clarence needed. His son Harry followed him, for another twenty-nine years, until 1975.[6]

In the 1980s, Clarence regulars conceived the idea of a Hastings Pub Quiz League. The pub itself had a successful team that beat several other teams in the town. The four members were landlord Richard Gillett, Arthur Downer, Bob Ivey and John Hodges who between them answered hundreds of questions and got 98% correct. John Hodges says: 'I have been a member of many quiz teams, some at a national level, some throughout the south-east, some in Sussex and Kent and some just around Hastings. We have won competitions at all levels. The Clarence was our base for the first national pubs' quiz competition. I think that was in 1985.'[7]

However, within the league there was dissent. Some of the thirty-two teams were unhappy about the type of questions they had to cope with. The landlord of the Carlisle commented that it was more like a Brain of Britain quiz. There was also some interference by Charrington's brewery, who wanted the final to be held in one of its own pubs. Richard Gillet said at the time: 'We naturally must take guidance from them, it is only politically prudent for us to do so.'

Richard and Di Gillet moved to the Dripping Spring in the 1990s and the Clarence is now known as The Clarence@Silverhill.

Clifton Tavern
Stainsby Street

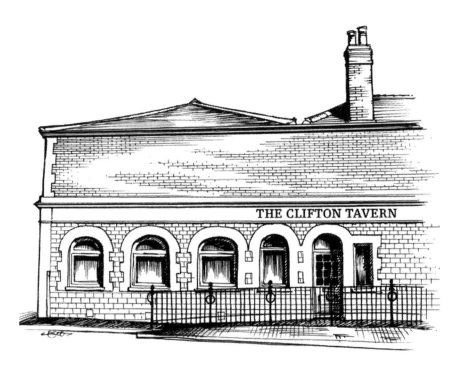

This pub, on the north side of Warrior Square railway station, was granted a spirit licence in 1870, but was a beer house before then.[1] The first landlord was James Brockhill who stayed until 1888. During his time he encouraged several organisations to use the pub on a regular basis. In 1895 eighty members of the newly organised Hastings and St Leonards Branch of the Postmen's Federation held their first annual general meeting here. They decided issues such as a minimum wage for postmen of £2 per week, pensions and 'gratuity insurance'.[2]

The St Leonards branch of the Buffaloes, which had seventy-three members,[3] also held weekly meetings and before the First World War the Clifton had its own Benefit Society, which organised 'Smoking Concerts' and musical programmes. One such concert in 1913, entertained with renditions of 'Drake Goes West' [encore], 'My Sporting Guide', Ragtime piano and comic recitations by 'The Three Freds'. On another evening it raised £14 for the local hospital. Using the historic retail price index, £14 in 1913 is worth £958 today![4]

In 1916, during the First World War, the potman, Alfred Winder, aged forty, was called up into the army. He appealed to the Hastings Military Tribunal, on the basis that his aged mother relied on the 14s [70p] a week he gave her. Their situation was ignored, exemption was refused and he was sent off to fight in France. It is not known whether he returned.

In the 1920s, the landlord applied to extend closing time by half an hour to 10.30pm, during July, August and September. Several customers, who were members of the St Leonards Allotments Association, worked on their allotments late on summer evenings and looked forward to a pint after heavy digging. They accompanied the landlord to the magistrates court to lend their support. However, there was no change and the 10pm closing time stayed.[5] Although members of the SLAA socialised in the Clifton, they possibly held Association meetings here as well. The SLAA still exists and has a long local history.

From 1907 until 1938, the Clifton's longstanding landlord was E.C. Bannister, who was awarded a silver tea set on his retirement. Some customers, who used the pub when he took over, were still there when he retired. One said: 'I always thought "Dr" Bannister's medicine kept me young and healthy'. Another customer had been drinking at the pub since 1886 and attended the landlord's wedding.

During the Second World War, customers not called up were still active on their allotments 'digging for victory'. In the evenings they played darts and won the *Observer* Annual Darts Tournament three years running, from 1942 to 1944, beating all other Hastings pub teams. The prizes were National Savings Certificates.[6] The chief constable opposed an application for a music licence in 1942. 'I'm not having this class of public house turned into a community singing hall', he said.[7]

In 1945 they were still digging for victory and supported the Hastings Food Production Exhibition attended by 15,000 people at White Rock. The main exhibit was entitled Dawn of Peace, in a design of red and yellow tomatoes, against a background of potatoes, with the words: '1939–1945 Victory. Thank you', in runner beans. All were grown from seeds donated by America.[8]

Customers were still winning at darts in 1970, when the Clifton Ladies' Team beat all other ladies' teams in the Watney's Games League. Around 500 people gathered in the ballroom on Hastings pier to watch them receive their trophy.

During the entire lifetime of the Clifton, there does not seem to have been any recorded incident of drunkenness, bad behaviour or serving out of hours. Literally, pub life on the other side of the railway track seemed to be a long way from that of some other pubs. But all good things must come to an end and in the 1980s the Clifton was let down by the Phoenix Brewery, and licensees Wally and Enid Beerling threatened to sue them for poor maintenance.

In 1986, one regular, Winnie Suckling, who had been drinking there since the 1920s, was presented with a set of glass goblets and guaranteed a free drink every day for the rest of her life. The pub closed in the 1990s and although it didn't become a 'community singing hall' it did become a community centre! Its name and sign, an impression of the Clifton suspension bridge in Bristol, were painted directly onto the front wall and are still visible.

Clive Vale Hotel
Old London Road, Ore

From the 1870s there were several applications for new licences for premises on the Clive Vale Estate in the north-east district of Hastings. One was for a proposed twelve-bedroom hotel, 'to be erected at the junction of Alfred Road and the Old London Road', on a plot of land set aside for a new public house by the British Land Company. The application, opposed by the Hare and Hounds, was refused at least five times but was finally granted in 1886 to William Luck, previously landlord of the Millers Arms.[1]

The British Land Company dated back to the 1850s. Its policy was to acquire building land that could be divided into plots. Ownership of a house on one of these plots qualified men to vote, through the 'forty-shilling freehold'.[2]

The pub had a variety of customers in its early years. In the 1890s the Clive Vale Bicycle Club met here, as did a branch of the Equitable Friendly Society and the Ore and Clive Vale Rifle, Bowls and Quoits Club. In 1909 this club celebrated a 'quoits handicap on the American system, on their enlarged and improved ground' beside the pub in Alfred Road.[3] This club was still going strong in 1920.[4] The Clive Vale was one of the few pubs where quoits was played in Hastings, although the Edinburgh Castle on the West Hill had a quoits club, as did the Norman in St Leonards. There may have been other pub teams. Hastings Borough Council provided facilities for the game in Alexandra Park in 1911 and the current Alexandra and Clive Vale Bowls Club stems from that time. The game was played outside by throwing metal rings down a pitch at target pins embedded in the ground.

By 1915 the pub was showing middle class credentials by hosting suppers for the All Souls Church Choir and for the local cricket club. But in the 1920s its social base began to change and by the depression of the 1930s it was a popular pub with 'webbers', men who drove rabbits into long webbed nets, placed at right angles along two sides of a field. A successful night's webbing could produce up to 150 rabbits, that were then sold in the community and in the pub.

In an interview with Hastings Local History Group, Tom Blackman (1915–1981), an old customer, recalled: 'I can remember them all that used to come here. And one pub in particular called the Clive Vale, it's still there, but altered now, and if you went in that pub on Sunday dinner time, it's no exaggeration, in them days there were a row of seats all the way round, and they used to sit there, and you didn't dare put your foot under the seat, because there'd be about twenty dogs lying under there. And there'd be rabbits and everything else in that pub. And them dogs the breeding wasn't worth four pence as the saying is but them dogs was worth their weight in gold ... they'd watch one hole for you and if the rabbit came out they'd grab it, and if the ferret come out they'd squeak and tell you the ferret was out.'

He continued, 'They weren't actual poachers because poaching is when you take game. It was quite an honourable profession in them days ... you never looked down on a rabbit catcher. If you got caught the charge was: "trespassing in search of conies". It was just a way of life: they lived rabbits, talked rabbits and hunted rabbits. Things were so hard that a few rabbits meant everything ... And they say the good old days!'[5]

In 1987 the pub changed its name to Brunel's and in an advert, a piece of pure marketing hype, the Clive Vale gave itself some false history:

'Originally named the Railway, this pub was designed by Isambard Kingdom Brunel in 1886 as a small hotel outside the proposed site of Ore railway station. In the event the railway engineers couldn't blast through the rock and Ore Station was resited where it is today. It was renamed the Clive Vale Hotel.'[6]

The fallacy of this statement is self evident. Firstly, engineers wouldn't build a railway uphill when they could follow the Ore Valley and secondly, the local rock is Hastings sandstone. Furthermore, the pub was never known as the Railway and Brunel had nothing to do with the Clive Vale Hotel, Ore railway station or the South Eastern Railway.

The idea comes from a mistaken belief in the Ore community, that the Clive Vale Hotel was a folly erected in anticipation of Ore railway station being built nearby. The fact that Francis Thompson, an architect who worked for Brunel, lived in Alfred Road in the early 1900s, most probably influenced this idea.

The name Brunel's lasted only twelve months before it was renamed again as the New Clive Vale, in 1988.[7] After an active century the Clive Vale closed soon after.

Clown
Russell Street

The Clown claims the title of 'Hastings's cosiest pub' and it is certainly one of the smallest. It was probably named after the famous clown, Joseph Grimaldi (1779 –1837).

In the *Hastings Directory* for 1885, the building is listed as a beer house and probably a shop, located near the Gaiety Music Hall (now the Odeon Cinema). It became known as the Clown in 1888 and the first landlord was J.H. Vidler.[1]

In 1905, immediately after the 1904 Licensing Act came into force, the Clown was nominated by the chief constable, along with twenty-four other Hastings pubs, for closure on the grounds that it was 'no longer required' and should be made redundant. He claimed that 'the premises were such that no magistrate would grant a new licence'.[2]

However, the locals who drank there attended the licensing sessions and put up a rigorous defence. One of them described it as 'a round the corner sort of place with respectable customers'. The Clown was reprieved, but the magistrates closed down five other pubs that year.

Eight years later, in 1913, Edwin Turner, an old army man 'invalided out after six years in the colours', bought the business, still a simple beer house, from Smith's Lamberhurst Brewery. It must have been a successful business, for nine years later in 1922 he bought the freehold for £755, which in 2006, using the historic retail price index, was equivalent to £28,000. This made him, at that time a rare person in Hastings, the owner of a free house.[3]

The licence was opposed again by the chief constable in 1928 but the pub was reprieved a second time, as it was not possible to compensate a free house with money from the brewery. On examination it was found that trade was not large, but as a free house the Clown sold the 'better beers', where the profit margin was proportionally greater and perhaps three times that of ordinary mild ale. The Clown was basically a single bar divided into two and the jug and bottle (a beer takeaway) was the smallest in Hastings measuring only 7 feet 7 inches by 4 feet 8 inches [2.3m by 1.4m].[4]

In 1930 the licence was opposed for a third time and the pub's regulars went back to court to protest yet again. 'It's a restful little place', they said, 'it's a shame to take it away from us'. The Licensed Victuallers Association pointed out that the landlord had a good record. He had previously been landlord of the Black Horse, Halton and had 'never had an upset in fifteen years'. Again it stayed open.[5]

The Clown seems to have remained open during the years of the Second World War, when it entered a team in the *Observer* Darts Tournament. The Clown was (and is) a working class pub and most of its competition came from the Castle Shades, the Gaiety and the York Tavern (all now closed), the Central Hotel (now Moda, which caters for a younger customer) and the Bedford, which was bombed in 1940.

The Clown's trade has always increased in the summer months. In the 1890s it was popular with 'excursionists' who travelled to Hastings by train. By the 1930s they had become 'day trippers', travelling to Hastings by charabanc from London. They often loaded up with crates of beer for the return journey. Cricket fans who came for the matches across the road on the Central Cricket Ground were also good customers.

In 1949 the Clown was granted a licence for the consumption of wine on and off the premises, ending its sixty-four years as a beer house,[6] followed by a full licence in 1954.[7] Two years later, in 1956, an early case of racial violence and abuse occurred. One evening three young men walked into the Clown and abused and assaulted an ethnic seaman, who was on his own, playing darts. The youths were ejected, arrested, charged and fined. But the magistrate's racism was even worse than the accused. However, a witness pointed out that 'the attitude of the crowd who gathered outside the pub showed that they were prepared to take the part of the coloured man'.[8]

One regular in the 1990s was Roger Povey, who chatted with the young barman living in the Clown at the time. The barman claimed that one morning after a busy night, he came down into the bar and seeing what a mess it was, decided, after a cup of coffee, to start clearing up. When he returned he found it thoroughly cleaned, with the brass tabletops polished. He put this down to the resident ghost.[9]

More recently one drinker warned to be wary of the arm wrestling Welsh lady in the crop top. She wrestles anyone for a pint and always wins.

Cricketers

South Terrace

The Cricketers was first licensed in 1864.[1] Its most famous customer was Robert Tressell, author of *The Ragged Trousered Philanthropists,* a novel set in Hastings, incorporating the 'Labour Theory of Value'. Tressell drank here in the early years of the twentieth century and this was the pub where he observed the drinkers who became the prototypes for the characters of the Semi-drunk and the Besotted Wretch.[2] The description of the Cricketers which follows is paraphrased from Tressell's book.

The pub was arranged in five bars. There was a saloon bar, a jug and bottle for taking away beer and two private bars, with room only for two or three people looking for 'four pennyworth of spirits'. These private bars were 'much appreciated by ladies, who liked to indulge in a drop of gin on the quiet'. Finally there was the much larger public bar, with sawdust and spittoons.

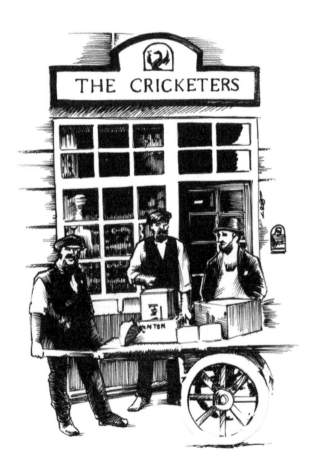

In the public bar a 'large automatic instrument', a polyphone, (an antique music player with a cylinder, a forerunner of the jukebox,) stood close to the counter. Nearby was a ring board, about fifteen inches [38cm] square, where players threw rubber rings onto numbered hooks, and a shove penny board, played with old French pennies kept behind the bar. Above it a neatly printed framed notice said:

> *Gentlemen using this house are*
> *respectfully asked to refrain*
> *from using obscene language.*

'The landlord was a well fed and prosperous looking individual, in a fancy waistcoat, gold watch chain and a diamond ring. The landlady was a large woman with a highly coloured countenance ... a large bust encased in a black dress and several gold rings on her fat, white hands.'

One of the regulars, 'a shabbily dressed, bleary eyed, degraded, beer sodden, trembling wretch', spent the greater part of every day and all of his money in this bar. He was a miserable looking wreck of a man about thirty, but was a very good customer.

The other main regular was a shabby, semi-drunken man in a bowler hat with a 'very thin, pale face and a large high bridged nose, bearing a striking resemblance to the first Duke of Wellington'.

'Wotcher', said the landlord affably, greeting the customers, 'Ow goes it?' 'All reet me ole dear', was the usual reply. 'Well wot's it to be.' 'Ere's the skin orf yer nose' was the usual toast. The landlord would put a penny in the polyphone and it would start to play. The Semi-drunk would rise to his feet unsteadily and begin shuffling and singing:—

> *'They may build their ships, my lads,*
> *And try to play the game,*
> *But they can't build the boys of the Bulldog breed,*
> *Wot made ole Hingland's—'*

'Ere! Stop that, will yer?' cried the Old Dear, fiercely. 'I told you once before that I don't allow that sort of thing in my   ouse!'
'I didn't mean no   arm', he said unsteadily, appealing to the company.

'I don't want no chin from you!' said the Old Dear with a ferocious scowl. 'If you want to make that row you can go somewheres else, and the sooner you goes the better. You've been ere long enough.'

Tressell observed the pub games, the Besotted Wretch throwing the rubber rings at the ring board. The customers laughed when he missed and applauded 'when he threw a good ring'.

On one occasion he watched the two regulars play each other. 'You can't play for nuts', said the Besotted Wretch. 'Can't I? I can play you, anyway.' 'Right you are! I'll play you for a round!' cried the Semi-drunk. 'Come on then. What's it to be? Fifty up?' 'Anything you like! Fifty or a 'undred or a bloody million!'

'Holding the six rings in his left hand, the man stood in the middle of the floor at a distance of about three yards. Taking one of the rings between the forefinger and thumb of his right hand and closing his left eye, he carefully "sighted" the centre hook, then he slowly extended his arm to its full length then, bending his elbow, he brought his hand back again until it nearly touched his chin, and slowly extended his arm again. He repeated these movements several times, whilst the others watched with bated breath. Getting it right at last he suddenly shot the ring at the board, but instead of hooking on No 13, it went over the partition into the private bar' to the huge delight of the watching customers.[3]

Ninety years later, there was a series of problems with flooding. In 1992 the Cricketers was flooded five times and after the Environmental Health Department had condemned its cellar, the pub closed down for a time. In 1995, the cricket ground opposite was redeveloped into Priory Meadow Shopping Centre and construction work brought complaints of cloudy beer. Sediment in the barrels was disturbed by the vibration caused by pile driving and turned the beer cloudy, making it unsaleable.

In 1996 it became the Priory and then the Jazz and Blues House. It is now a gambling venue called the Hastings Terrace Club.

Crown Inn
All Saints Street, Old Town

The original Crown Inn was situated in nearby Courthouse Street and dated from the sixteenth century. There has been a pub on the current site since 1794, when it was a coaching inn licensed to William Smith and then to his widow Sarah Smith from 1815 to 1832.[1]

In the early nineteenth century, the Crown and the nearby Swan Inn were described as 'the principal rendezvous of gentility'. As early as 1817, Hastings was so crowded in the summer months that the Crown had its loft fitted up as sleeping quarters for the servants and engaged up to thirty other beds off the premises.[2]

Coaches set off for London, Brighton and Dover from here. An advert in 1816 said: 'The Crown Inn coach sets off every morning at 8am and arrives in London at 6pm. It is driven by the most experienced coachman.'[3]

Powell's Hastings Guide for 1831 says Mrs. Smith 'deserves particular commendation and support, as being the first (with a family of seven children) to add to the accommodation of visitors by every species of comfort, neatness, and domestic attention'.[4]

In 1835 John Sawyer, a butcher, became landlord and brought one of his employees, Sam Barwell, with him. Barwell's main occupation was driving cattle and he supervised large herds of 'beeves' in the nearby slaughterhouses. Tending the bar was a secondary occupation.

By the 1840s, when the commercial centre of Hastings was moving west, the Crown began to lose its fashionable status and became a minor tavern. By the 1850s the Crown, like the Old Town itself, took on a different, more common character with its various landlords, often appearing in court either charged with, or as witness to, various undesirable activities that took place in its bars, parlours and taproom.

A typical example is seen in the Crown on an evening in the 1850s. A 'preventive man' [customs officer] had his purse stolen while having a quiet drink in the bar. The purse was eventually retrieved from a woman's bosom, empty, after she tried to swap it for a glass of gin. On another occasion a constable heard 'indecent, noisy language' coming from the Crown and found five men and seven 'girls on the town', in a side parlour. One of them asked him to have a brandy, and a butcher, who was having supper in a little back parlour, admitted there were some 'improper characters' in the bar.[5]

Around the same time, an Irishman known as Old Jack was buried at All Saints Church. A wake was held in the Crown and it was reported that 'everyone was thoroughly inebriated and set the neighbourhood in an uproar with their strange freaks'.[6] In 1856 a German, who lodged at the Crown, was also buried at All Saints', after cutting his throat. A German band played the Death March.[7]

Like most Old Town pubs, the Crown was next door to a common lodging house, where on one occasion, a man had his dinner (a sheep's head) stolen by a customer. On at least two occasions the landlord was charged with running a 'disorderly house' and fined. One customer used counterfeit coinage and the pub itself was unlicensed for a time, but it was never closed down.

After nearly fifty years the situation improved. A large Buffaloes Lodge was formed here in the 1890s. Their meetings raised Primo members to 'degrees of knighthood', where they drank each other's health dressed in Buffalo regalia.[8] In 1898 the All Saints' Conservative Association held social evenings here and in 1900, when the Boer War broke out, a large gathering of local dignitaries gathered to give patriotic, nationalistic and jingoistic support to the local volunteers who had been dispatched to South Africa.[9]

In 1905 the annual dinner of the All Saints' Football Club was held here. The club was the winner of all three Carlisle, Rye and Hastings League Cups. During this period, this once large inn, now known as Ye Olde Crown House, was reduced in size and in 1911 the licensee, A.J. Littlejohn, went bankrupt. The following year he was working on the Titanic as a bar steward. When the ship sank he escaped in lifeboat thirteen.

In 1921, a serious fire destroyed the building and Watney's rebuilt the pub we see today.[10] In 1984 the Crown became Harvey's first Hastings pub and closed for a year for refurbishment.

Landlord A.J. Littlejohn

Cutter

East Parade

The Cutter was built in 1769 and rebuilt thirty-seven years later, as a ship-lap timber building in the centre of the Hastings fishing industry.[1] James Bell was landlord from 1807 to 1823, when the pub had a sign which read 'Ship representing a Cutter' and 'James Bell, dealer in Ale. Bottled 4d'. During the Napoleonic Wars he was a valet to Lord Nelson.[2]

In 1813, the Cutter became the first meeting place of the Derwent Lodge of the Freemasons. Alfred Chatfield, formerly a footman and then a barber, became landlord around 1840. In 1860 the poet and Pre-Raphaelite painter, Dante Gabriel Rossetti, stayed here before marrying Elizabeth Siddal in St Clements Church. The sight of the sun sinking in the west over the Hastings coast left an impression on him. His stay is recorded on a blue plaque.

The Poet and Painter
DANTE GABRIEL
ROSSETTI
(1828 - 1882)

Stayed here during 1860
Prior to his wedding
On 23rd May, 1860
at nearby
St Clement's Church

O.H.P.S.

A popular drink at the time was 'three pennyworth of rum and eggs', an early type of 'eggnog' served to upper middle class customers in the smoking room.[3]

During the last forty years of the nineteenth century, the Cutter followed the general decline of the Old Town and another class of customer began to turn up. In 1868 an engine driver fell asleep on a bench opposite the pub. Around 10pm, a woman called Elizabeth Evans woke him up asking: 'Will you stand me a drink?' This was a common approach used by prostitutes at the time. They went into the Cutter and called for a 'quartern of whisky', in a small room at the side of the bar. Later, he realised the woman had stolen four sovereigns [£4] from his pocket. A policeman later found her in the Royal Standard and she was arrested.[4]

In 1872, a costermonger was summonsed, for trying to obtain sixpence [2½p] by false pretences. He walked into the pub and asked for three ha'pennies [1p] worth of gin, for which he paid with a shilling [5p]. He said: 'Will you give me six coppers [2½p] for a sixpence piece?' The barmaid laid six coppers on the counter, but before she could pick up the coin, he asked for 'a shilling for a sixpenny piece and six coppers'. She gave him a shilling and he put a sixpenny piece on the counter, with the coppers. He attempted the same trick at the Hastings Arms, but was caught out. The police finally picked him up in the Alma, another Old Town pub long since disappeared.[5]

In 1876 two vegetable hawkers left their carts outside the pub, while they went inside to 'wet a deal'. When they came out one cart was gone, only later to be found in Eastbourne with 4 hundredweight [203kg] of potatoes missing. Other customers included fly drivers, grocers, fish buyers, butchers, marine store dealers and waiters, of whom the landlord sometimes complained of their 'picky' (i.e. bad) language.[6]

In the 1890s the Hastings and St Leonards Bicycle Club held their annual smoking concerts here and prizes were awarded for an annual '100 mile' ride to Worthing and back followed by a programme of songs and entertainment by a 'glee party'.[7]

The Cutter was rebuilt in 1927 and refurbished in 1957, when the house on the west side was added. When it reopened, the landlord, in the company of local fishermen and the lifeboat crew in oilskins, was presented with a painting of a cutter and the Hastings lifeboat was presented with a cheque by the brewery.

In his book *Fishermen of Hastings*, Steve Peak describes the 'Hastings Upper and Lower Lights as a centuries old navigation system for boats coming ashore. When boats at sea had the two lights in line they could turn inland into a safe channel between two ridges of rock.' In the nineteenth century the upper light was located at the top of Light Steps, George Street and the lower light was to the east of the Cutter.[8]

In the 1990s, the leaseholds of the Cutter and four other Hastings pubs were held by Ray Lee, who by 1995, owed a massive £20,000 to the brewery for beer supplied to the Cutter, the Norman, the Marina Fountain, the Royal George (later the Priory) and the Dolphin. Under pressure of debt, he suddenly left Hastings and absconded with his wife to South Africa.[9]

Dripping Spring
Tower Road, Bohemia

The triangle of land between Bohemia Road, Cornfield Terrace and Tower Road contains some of the earliest housing in Bohemia including, at one time, at least four pubs on Bohemia Road. In 1866 Richard Moy, landlord of one of them, the Prince of Wales, complained about the competition from 'two more beer houses in Bohemia'. One of these was the forerunner of the Dripping Spring, a grocer's shop and beer house run by Thomas Stubbenfield, at 35 Tower Road. Number 34, now the saloon bar, was a bootmakers.[1]

Stubbenfield's shop continued until 1899, but the beer house became separated from it in 1892, to become the Dripping Spring. Mrs Phoebe Tapp held the licence that year, but proved herself to be ill fitted for the life of a publican. In her first year she was fined for permitting drunkenness and her licence was revoked.[2] The next landlord was Sydney Smith, who remained until 1896.

Before the First World War, the Dripping Spring ran a slate club, which in 1909 paid out £1 7s 2d [£1.36] to each of seventy-six members. The club came to an end when its members were recruited into the military.

In 1915 the potman was called up into the 'territorials'. A short time later in 1916 the landlord, Fred Smith, was also called up. He appealed to the Hastings Military Tribunal and explained that he and his wife now ran the Dripping Spring alone. He did all the cellar work himself and explained that the lightest barrel was a quarter-hundredweight [12.7kg], the heaviest four and a quarter-hundredweight [218kg] and a two dozen crate of beer was a quarter-hundredweight. His appeal was refused and he was granted an exemption of one month only, before being sent to France.[3] After his departure his wife struggled on with help from the customers but Fred was lucky: he returned from France alive and well and remained landlord until 1921, when the 'Drip' was taken over by Charles Martin.

Charles Martin successfully applied for a wine licence in 1938 supported by a petition signed by 153 customers, although the Bohemia Arms, the Tower Hotel, the Prince of Wales and the chief constable opposed it.[4]

Unlike many pubs, the Drip stayed open during the Second World War and in 1940 the building was improved. In 1943 and 1944 the Drip entered two darts teams in the Annual *Observer* Darts tournament. It managed to escape the bombing, unlike the Tower Hotel, which had to remove a bomb from its cellar.

In 1950 the Dripping Spring was granted a full licence and its eighty-four years of life as a beer house came to an end. As the Licensing Act of 1910 stipulated that only pubs with two bars could have a full licence, the house next door was acquired and its ground floor turned into the saloon bar still in use today. Before this the entrance to the single bar was on the corner of Cornfield Terrace. In the same year it was included in the Whitbread inn signs series.[5]

Cyril Pelluet remembers the pub from 1957. 'Sometimes we went to the Dripping Spring', he says, 'which we considered a better quality pub. The inside was smarter and husbands and wives went there together. Wives just didn't go to the Prince of Wales or the Bohemia Arms. The Dripping Spring was a bit higher up the social scale. Not very far up but just a bit'.[6]

In 1992 the Dripping Spring became a free house and was known as the New George and Dragon, until 1995.[7] It started selling real ale in 1994 and in 1995 was listed in the *Good Beer Guide*. In 2000, the pub was voted CAMRA Sussex Pub of the Year and also runner-up as National Pub of the Year, to become the second best CAMRA pub in the country. The pub was listed in the *Good Beer Guide* for ten years from 1997 to 2007 and again in 2009.

The pub is located on a part of Tower Road once known as Spring Terrace. The area is said to have several springs, one of which is thought to flow in a culvert beneath the pub cellar. Why or where it drips is a mystery. The present sign dates from 2008. The previous sign, now in the back garden, portrays a 'dandy' with a cane and a glass of wine, standing by a spring, location unknown.

First In Last Out
High Street, Old Town

From 1854 to 1869 a poor beer house was located in Waterloo Passage, a twitten alongside the building which is now the FILO. In the latter year, its licence was revoked because the premises were 'insufficiently rated'. Landlord William Oakley said: 'This is a hard case especially after I kept it fifteen years. The rating was high enough until the Rating Committee put it down!'

In the same year the building, which now houses the FILO, was a corn dealer's, run by one Charles Pearson.[1] In 1876 he started selling beer and by 1880 the premises had been transformed into a beer house.[2] George Crampton took over in 1889 and gave the First In Last Out its distinctive name. He remained landlord until 1901 before moving to the newly licensed Railway Stores, Hughenden Road, near Ore Station.[3] He left the FILO owing money to a local beer wholesaler, which suggests that he didn't brew beer himself.

Before the First World War, the FILO ran two very successful slate clubs, one for men and one for women. The fact that it had a female club suggests it had female customers, which was advanced for that time. We know that many pubs were negative about female custom and, in the majority of cases, women were not served. The slate clubs met regularly to organise sick, unemployment and death benefits and for social occasions and dinners. In 1909, for example the men's slate had thirty-three members and paid out £40 1s 9d [£40.08] in sick pay.[4]

Twenty years later, the chief constable claimed that there were too many pubs in the Old Town and attempted to close down the FILO. The landlord, Samuel Mepham, was accused of being drunk in charge of the bar and it seemed a foregone conclusion that the pub would close.

However, the case was unusual. The landlord had served in France in the First World War and claimed to suffer from 'neurasthenia', a condition brought about by trench gas in the Somme. He had also suffered a kick in the head by an army horse and these two things, he claimed, were the cause of his depression, strange appearance and unusual behaviour. Although he had medical witnesses, the court obviously disbelieved his story and fined him two guineas [£2.10] This was in July 1929 and by August he had lost his licence, which was temporarily transferred to a manager of Ballard's Brewery Lewes.[5] The police then stopped opposing the licence 'having no further evidence to offer against renewal' and the life of the FILO continued.[6] This brought the total number of landlords between 1908 and 1929 to eight.

The FILO slate club was still very active and by then had fifty-eight members, including several men over fifty years of age A second argument put forward to the magistrates was that if the pub closed, these members would not be able to join any other slate club because of their age and would lose their benefits. FILO regulars Arthur Wood, Albert Colbran, George Jackson and George Gallop, among others, appeared as witnesses for both the pub and the slate club. Arthur Wood described the FILO as 'a nice little house which doesn't pretend to be a Gin Palace'. The FILO was reprieved with a new landlord.

David Harding in the St Clement's brewery in 1986

In 1933 the FILO applied for a wine licence. The landlord told the magistrates that he was interested in promoting 'the wines of the British Empire', which was bringing 'wine within reach of the middle and working classes' for the first time. However, a wine licence was refused[7] and the FILO had to wait another twenty years before it could legally sell wine. After seventy-eight years as a beer house, the pub was granted a full licence in 1954.[8] It has been a free house since 1976, having previously been tied to Charrington's.

In 1982, the FILO acquired a milk pump and was the first (and only) Hastings pub to sell pints of draught milk.[9] Four years later the St Clements micro-brewery was established on the premises, using four milk pasteurising tanks, by landlord David Harding. This was three years after a micro-brewery was established at Mr Cherry's on the Marina, although the brewery at the FILO is still operating.

In 2001 the brewery was updated and modernised and currently produces Crofters Best Bitter, Cardinal (Sussex Porter), Ginger Tom and Filo Gold (Premium Ale) and also occasional beers for special events such as bonfire night. The FILO has appeared in the *Good Beer Guide* over several years and it has been home to the Hastings branch of the Society for the Preservation of Beers in the Wood.

The pub name possibly comes from the game of cricket or from the fact that it was, at one time, the last pub before Halton. The pub sign shows a stage coach. The pub logo displays a silhouette of a cat at night.

The FILO End of Summer Festival

on Fri 13th, Sat 14th & Sun 15th Oct

FEATURING

Friday 13th
Steve Winchester and Andy Neate

Saturday 14th
Bo'ville
Roger Hubbard

Sunday 15th
Liane Carroll

plus other guest performers

First In Last Out
14/15 High Street
Old Town, Hastings
(01424) 425079

Appearing on all 3 Days

WADWORTH'S
Malt & Hops

MANSFIELD'S
Old Bailey

ARCHER'S
Best Bitter

ASH VINE'S
Challenger

BUNCES
Best Bitter

HOGS BACK'S
T.E.A.

HOOK NORTON'S
Old Hookey

HOP BACK'S
Summer Lightning

SUMMERSKILLS
Indiana Bones

FILO'S
Crofters & Cardinal

THEAKSTON'S
Old Peculier

Guest Appearance DRAUGHT "BUDVA"

1995

Foresters Arms
Shepherd Street

The building of St Leonards in the 1830s required a large workforce, many of whom were itinerant travelling tradesmen who had found accommodation on America Ground, Hastings. America Ground was an area of unowned land on the Hastings shoreline inhabited by a large community who had raised the Stars and Stripes as a symbol of their independence.

The 'Americans' were evicted in 1835 and a large number of them moved to St Leonards, taking their homes with them. One 'American', Daniel Thomas, was landlord of an old gin house named the Black Horse, on the site of what is now Holy Trinity Church in Hastings town centre.

The Black Horse was dismantled and re-erected in Shepherd Street, St Leonards, by James (Jemmy) Hyland.[1] Many of the original buildings from America Ground still stand in the surrounding streets.

For most of the nineteenth century, the Black Horse was both a beer house and a small, crowded lodging house where, if you weren't careful, you would find your belongings in a nearby second-hand shop. Lodgers slept two to a bed. One evening a policeman checking on closing time found the ground floor empty but insisted on going upstairs, where he found six men drinking beer from earthenware pots in a room with three beds.

In the 1850s some customers spent all day here drinking and playing 'Four Corners'.[2] This was a game played by throwing a large wooden bowl or 'cheese' weighing 6 to 8 lbs [2.7 to 3.6 kg], at four large pins placed at the corners of a square frame, from a distance of about 10 feet [3m]. Because of the space required, it was usually played in a Four Corners shed, which must have been in a rear outbuilding. Customers at this time included the railway navvies, building the line through to Hastings.[3]

In 1864 the Black Horse hit the headlines when there was an 'Attempt at Murder and Arson'. Thomas Bowsteed of Gensing Road was charged with shooting William Tew with a pistol and of trying to set fire to a workshop behind the pub that Tew rented from the landlord.

Tew said: 'I was shot from behind. I staggered and fell and walked away down Valentine's Passage'. Then the landlord's eleven-year-old son discovered a burning candle placed on a pile of wood

A game of Four Corners in 1856
Note the man sitting down is smoking a 'Churchwarden',
a 2 feet long clay pipe, popular at the time.

shavings in the workshop, which he quickly put out. These charges 'excited considerable interest in the Hastings court, which was crowded daily'. The case was referred to Lewes Assizes and Bowsteed was imprisoned for several years.[4]

In the 1870s the landlord, George Earle, 'an elderly man with a wooden leg', was cautioned for allowing late night drinking. In his defence he said that one man found on the premises by the police was a cellarman who came in every night to tap the barrels, because 'I only have one beer engine'. He couldn't do it himself because he 'couldn't stoop and if the tap busted, beer flew all over the bar'. Another man, George Copley, a lodger, said he 'had some beer drawn but it was so full of froth he wouldn't pay for it'. The case was dismissed with a warning that 'it is unusual to tap beer this time of night'. The court was attended by several of George's customers including an artistic decorator, a grainer and a shoesmith.[5]

Before the arrival of the railway St Leonards had its ice, coal, timber, building materials and other goods delivered by boat onto the beach opposite the end of London Road. Some of these boats often arrived late on Saturday night or early Sunday morning, when pubs were supposed to be closed. A provision in the law allowed pubs to serve 'bona fide travellers' including boat crews, outside of normal hours, but this did not include the men who unloaded the boats. When the boats were in, police often checked with a knock on the door. 'Who've you got in the kitchen, lodgers?' 'No', said the landlord, 'men working on the collier just come ashore', and got into trouble for it.

Between 1886 and 1888 the Black Horse was rebuilt and renamed the Foresters Arms.[6] In 1905 the chief constable tried to get the Foresters closed down and the magistrates questioned Breeds Brewery on the need to keep it open. In the rear yard, a cottage was let at 4s 6d [22½p] a week and three workshops at 6d [2½p] a week each. These were reached by a twitten called Black Horse Passage, formerly Valentine's Passage, which had its own entrance.

At this time the landlord worked as an upholsterer during the day. The previous landlord had been an army pensioner and local bandmaster. The pub takings averaged £11 a week and the rent was £18 a year. They sold 204 barrels of beer a year and a lot of bread, cheese and pickles. One hundred loyal customers signed a memorial in support and the pub stayed open.[7]

A quarter of a century later, during the depression, a more upmarket landlord took over. He had been a steward at the Constitutional Club in Crowborough and licensee of the Sussex Hotel in Tunbridge Wells. In 1933 he applied for a wine licence, claiming that there was an all-year-round demand for wine in Shepherd Street.[8] This was refused and it was not until 1952 that the Foresters was granted a full licence.[9]

The last landlord was Eddy Churchill, who arrived in 1959. When he moved to a restaurant in Hastings in 1969, the Foresters closed its doors for the last time.[10] It was one of three Whitbread houses in St Leonards, including the Warrior's Gate and the British Queen. Originally, however, it was tied to St Leonard's Brewery which was situated next door in Shepherd Street. It is now a private house.

Fortune of War
Priory Road

During the Napoleonic Wars Halton, a district in the north-east of Hastings, was the site of a barracks for infantry, cavalry and artillery. The Fortune of War was built and opened in 1810 by Thomas Sinnock, to serve the troops.[1] About thirty years later, long after the troops had gone, this 'poorly constructed inn' had to be partly rebuilt and an old ice vault or 'tub hole' for depositing contraband spirits was discovered at the back of the pub. This indicated that the Fortune of War might have been an early rendezvous for local smugglers.[2]

After soldiers and smugglers came the railway navvies. The latter arrived in the 1850s to find work digging out the Ore tunnel and laying the track for the railway line to Ashford that now runs along the valley parallel to Priory Road.

The navvies were a law unto themselves and lived a hard and rough life. Many of them lived in tents and temporary huts alongside the line and were heavy drinkers. Landlords of the Fortune of War and other pubs were charged for serving 'out of hours' and for permitting drunkenness and disturbances on more than one occasion. The railway company engaged a chaplain, who attempted to get the number of pubs and licences reduced by lobbying the magistrates.[3]

Halton has always been a poor district and in 1885 the pub was the location of a coroner's inquest into a sad case of the suicide by drowning of a fish hawker, who lived around the corner and who had apparently been charged with cruelty to a horse. The evening before he died, the landlord of the Mount Pleasant Inn gave him a free pint. He was so poor he couldn't pay for it.

He simply left two sad letters. One was to a carman:—

Dear Sir, Please pay my wife the sum of ten shillings for a half hundredweight of wheel grease delivered this day. If you want any harness oil there is 2 or 3 gallons. I have instructed my wife to sell it to you for 4s per gallon. If you pay it you will do my family justice. Adieu

And the second letter to his wife:—

Madam, Please do the best you can as I have made up my mind to finish with this world at once. Take my little cart and keep it or sell it. Send to Mr Godden for 10s for the grease and if he wants any harness oil sell him the lot for 3s 6d a gallon. I am very sorry I can do no more. I have left my knife and glasses at the Duke of Cornwall, Winding Street, if you want them. They might be of use to you. J. Barton.[4]

In the 1890s the Fortune of War was a "Tory house' and several Conservative Smoking Concerts were held there around the turn of the century. It was here that the Conservatives organised the voting register of local working men. This part of Hastings, St Clement's Ward, was, in 1903, a marginal ward held by the Liberals, with only nine votes.[5]

The Liberals meanwhile held their meetings at the nearby Hope, a 'radical house', and often it seems both pubs held meetings on the same night. The Liberals offered radical beef pudding suppers, selections by the Cinque Ports Mandolin Band and discussions on Free Trade, an issue which the Conservatives saw as a cause of unemployment and the decline of British agriculture.[6]

The Fortune of War closed for a period in the First World War, under the restrictions of the Defence of the Realm Act, when the chief constable reported that the pub had given the Hastings police a lot of trouble and that it was frequented by large numbers of women. This was quite unusual, as most pubs at that time would not serve women on their own. However, many of its male customers had been called up into the army.

In 1963 Fremlin's Brewery attempted to transfer the licence to a suitable site on the Halton re-development scheme. The Fortune of War survived for another year before it was closed in 1964. By 1968 the magistrates had become impatient and wanted 'this terrible building out of the way'.[7] It was finally demolished in 1970 and the licence was transferred to the New Broom, on the Broomsgrove Estate. The New Broom later became the Malvern Tavern, now also closed.

There have been at least seven other 'lost' pubs in the Halton district: The Canteen, at Halton Barracks (1807–1823), the Baker's Arms (1860s), the Dun Horse, on Albion Street (1850–1912?), the Halton Tavern, Old London Road (1850s–1961) and the Hope, North Terrace (1835–1940s). There was also the Black Horse (1870s–1912) and Johnson's beer house (1870s), both in Priory Road.

In 1915 the landlord of the Hope was charged with allowing a woman to get drunk. When asked by the magistrate if she was sober he said: 'She was more sober than usual for Halton'. 'What do you mean?' asked the magistrate, 'are the people of Halton not generally sober?' The landlord replied: 'They all like a drop at times'.

With the closure of the Fortune of War the pub culture of Halton came to an end.

Fountain
Queens Road

The Fountain was first fully licensed in 1853.[1] At that time it stood at the northern extremity of the town, which was gradually spreading out from the centre. A memorial signed by fifty-four 'respectable residents' was presented to the licensing magistrates, in support of a full licence. The first landlord was Charles Edwards, who held the licence for twenty-nine years before selling up to the Hanbury Brewery in 1882.

Early customers of the Fountain public bar included the employees of Hastings gasworks, then on the opposite side of Queen's Road. Employment in the gasworks was laborious, hot and dirty work, leading many men into intoxication. When pub opening hours were regulated by the 1872 Licensing Act, the Fountain applied for extended hours to correspond with the shifts of the gasworks, but was refused.

Apart from the gasworks, this area was still partly rural and the slaughterhouses and pigsties, also across the road, were considered a great nuisance. It was reported that: 'Cattle on the roads, pig keeping and offal boiling were an offence to the ladies and invalids on their way to St Andrew's Park' (now Alexandra Park) 'and slaughtering effected property values.' However, according to G.D. Coleman, 'cattle and sheep were still being driven along Queen's Road to the slaughterhouse in Waterworks Road' as late as 1929.[2]

Slaughterhouse employees were also Fountain customers, as were the numerous horse dealers who, on coming into town to trade, tethered their animals nearby whilst they drank and completed transactions in the bar.

The butchers of Hastings had some sort of informal organisation in the town during these years and the Fountain, because of its location near the slaughterhouses, was known for a time as a 'butchers' pub'. In the 1870s butchers not only drank here but also used the pub for more formal occasions. In 1879, for example, thirty butchers attended a wedding party of one of their members at the Fountain. The party turned into a riotous celebration and the licensee was fined 10s [50p]. A waiter, Gabriel Eaton, was also cautioned.[3]

In 1916 during the First World War, landlord Sidney Faulkner was called up to serve in France. At the Hastings Military Tribunal in July of that year, he pointed out that he was in sole control of the Fountain and if it closed down, £500 investment would be lost. He was exempted by the military for two months before being sent off to fight.[4] At the end of the war the shop next door, in Stonefield Street, was incorporated into the pub to extend the saloon bar. The two separate bars still exist.

In 1937 the *Hastings Observer* 'put darts on the map in Hastings' when it organised the first Hastings Annual Darts Tournament. The

Fountain team came to brief fame when it reached the semi-final, where it was only narrowly beaten by the Hastings British Legion Club.

The match was held at the Cambridge (now the Tubman) and 'the room was packed with eager supporters of both teams, who watched the flight of the darts with an intensity not bettered at a test match'. The British Legion team admitted that: 'There were only two teams we feared, the Fountain and the Cambridge'.[5] But little did they fear the immediate future. Three years later the town was evacuated during the Battle of Britain and the Fountain closed down from 1940 until 1943.

In 1950 the Fountain sign was included in Whitbread's miniature inn sign series.[6] The present sign dates from when Shepherd Neame purchased the freehold in 1993.

Fox
North Street, St Leonards.

Formerly known as the British Queen, the Fox has had a chequered history. It was listed in the *Sussex Directory* of 1855 as a beer house and most likely existed before then.[1] The first landlord was James Barnett, who had his own pewter mugs inscribed 'J.B. British Queen, St Leonards'. These were probably used only in the saloon bar. Beer in the other bars was served in enamelled earthenware pots in quarts [2 pints], pints and half pints. In 1858 he moved on to become landlord of the Tivoli Tavern in Silverhill and in later years the pewter tankards became collectors items.[2]

George Linton applied for a full licence in 1862 but was refused, although his name appears in the licensees' register from 1865 to 1897 and the name of his widow Ann Linton from 1898 to 1909.[3] The pub was originally tied to the long gone St Leonards Brewery of Shepherd Street and has passed through the hands of seven different brewers since.

As a tenant of the St Leonards Brewery it sold the original 'St Leonards Pale Ale', brewed by them over 150 years ago. In the 1880s the British Queen sold its own whisky in bottles of its own design, which on at least one occasion was found by an inspector to be very much under proof.

In the 1890s the British Queen had problems with bookmakers and their 'runners' collecting bets in the bar, and landlady Ann Linton was cautioned for allowing them access to the premises. The runners in question worked for George Talbot, who kept a furniture shop at 10 North Street and collected betting slips from hotels, pubs and cafes.[4]

In the 1930s the British Queen was a popular darts venue, used by London General Omnibus employees residing at the Capel le Ferne convalescent home.[5] Ralph Peacock, formerly captain of the darts team, became landlord in 1938. In 1939 Whitbread completely refurbished the pub. The five bars and a private room were converted into three bars, large enough, it was claimed, for 100 customers. The doors were grained, leaded windows were fitted and the latest Coalite stoves were installed.

Along with the usual pub games, a new game of 'bull', played after the style of shove-penny, was installed.[6] Bull was played on an extended board with an extra bed, the tenth bed, containing the bull. 'Shove-penny, as opposed to shove-ha'penny', says Alan Crouch, 'was a game found only in Hastings and Eastbourne. The difference between the two was only in the coins used. Some players cheated by keeping a chestnut in their pocket. Rubbing the nut and then the penny affected its performance, as the oil in the nut made the penny stick. Shovepenny boards were treated with paraffin, water or beer and cleaned with newspaper or a beer mat. Players prepared the pennies by heating one up and putting it onto a block of wood, which made a mould. A cold penny was put into the mould and smoothed with emery cloth or a surface grinder. This enabled players to have pennies of different weights, giving each coin its own characteristics. However, before matches all pennies were weighed.'[7]

In 1940 the British Queen darts team won the Annual *Observer* Darts Tournament, beating fifty-four other pub teams.[8] However, this record was marred in 1942 when the next landlord, Stanley Wood, was summonsed for 'harbouring' army clothing, Canadian cigarettes and tobacco, which he was selling from behind the bar. In court it was stated he had 'ten pairs of woollen drawers, vests, socks, boots and other clothing all marked War Department'. He also had in his possession 6,680 Canadian cigarettes and 7lbs [3kg] of tobacco. He claimed to have lent money to Canadian soldiers, who offered the goods as security. He was fined £50 and lost his licence.[9]

Thirty-five years later the British Queen welcomed customers from another Commonwealth country. Michael Monk, a regular at the time, says: 'The Seychelles Islands gained independence from Britain in 1976. In 1977 or 1978, the Commonwealth Conference was being held in London. Among the delegates, the first president of the Seychelles, James Mancham, learned that he had been deposed by a coup d'état. Obviously he couldn't go back immediately and he and his delegation stayed in Hastings until it was safe to return. I don't know where they stayed but five or six ministers of the Seychelles Islands' government drank in the British Queen saloon bar for a couple of years and we spent many an evening in their company. It was quite friendly and relaxed and there was never any question of racism or anything like that. They must have eventually returned.'[10]

From the 1960s to the 1980s the custom of the British Queen was boosted by employees of the Central Electricity Generating Board, then a nationalised company, employed on the construction of the two power stations at Dungeness. Many lodged in St Leonards and were bussed daily to the site. The first power station was connected to the National Grid in 1965.[11]

The Fox has managed to stay open for over 160 years, although it did close down in 1990. After another refurbishment, when its three bars became two and the original pub sign of Queen Bodicea driving her chariot was taken down, it reopened in 1992 as the Fox. A new sign showing a fox was erected in 2009. The British Queen sign was included in Whitbread's miniature inn signs in 1950.[12]

French's Bar
Robertson Street

French's Bar was the first licensed premises in Robertson Street. It started life as the Royal Standard Hotel in 1851 and cost £1,500 to build. Eighty-seven local dignitaries, including many of Robertson Street's first shopkeepers, attended its opening dinner.

After a few months on a beer licence, it applied for a full licence.[1] A London barrister appeared out of courtesy to support the application at the brewster sessions, because the Victorian developers had stipulated that Robertson Street was 'available for trade purposes; but no taverns or public houses will be allowed without a special licence from the Crown Lessee'.[2] Permission was granted and its first landlord, Henry Baldock, received a full licence. Baldock stayed for only a short time. Between 1852 and 1854 it was known as the Priory Family Hotel, run by Mary and Anne Eldridge, after which it reverted back to the Royal Standard.[3]

In 1856, when Robertson Street was still being built, a series of vestry meetings was held at the Royal Standard (and also at the Wellington, now the Smugglers), in the parish of Holy Trinity, to discuss the possibility of building a new church. The land opposite was available for this purpose and a local aristocrat, Countess Waldgrave, offered to buy the site from the Crown. The church could have been built under a government act, but the vestry needed to find a parishioner willing to give legal notice to the bishop. No parishioner was willing to do this apparently, but the bishop agreed anyway. Donations totalling £2,486 were made and the church was built with local sandstone. In 1857, six years after the opening of the Royal Standard, the foundation stone of Holy Trinity was laid by the countess with a silver trowel and the church opened the following year.[4] A short time after this a drinking fountain dedicated to the countess was erected.

One evening in 1865, the Royal Standard held a raffle for 'a horse and chaise' which, most surprisingly, at a sovereign [£1] a ticket, proved a great attraction among the town's flymen (drivers of horse-drawn cabs). According to the historical retail price index, a sovereign in 1865 would, at today's values, be worth about £70.[5]

At this time the pub was also popular for sessions of 'hustling the hat', where each participant put a (marked) coin into a hat which was shaken and tipped out. All coins showing heads were withdrawn. The tails were put back into the hat and the process repeated. The final or 'true tail' had to pay for 'pots all round'. This was a popular custom with commercial travellers, summer visitors and locals but often ended in dispute. At least one court case resulted from this activity.[6] Other pubs that practiced 'hustling the hat' included the Tower Hotel in Bohemia.

Soon after, new owners Henry and Edward Kelsey, brewers from Tunbridge Wells, took over. They got rid of 'hustling the hat' but in the following year they had to deal with attempts to pass off counterfeit money. A scam by two London men was scuppered when a counterfeit shilling broke in half. After their arrest it was found they were carrying a lot of 'bad' money, most of it roughly cast from the same mould. They were both sent for trial at Lewes.[7]

In the 1920s French's was known as the Sussex Wine Stores. Later it was acquired by Henekey's and then in the 1970s, by Cinque Ports Hotels Limited.

Pat Dunn was a customer from the 1950s. 'Michael Trubshawe, a character actor and friend of David Niven, who had small parts in *The Guns of Navarone, The Pink Panther* and *A Hard Day's Night,* was landlord at the time', she says.[8]

In the 1990s the name changed to French's and in 1994 there was a claim by the licensee that 'French's was established in 1695' and an attempt was made to celebrate its 300th birthday. This was a marketing ploy and another example of a pub creating its own history, a piece of hype that was obviously inaccurate. In 1695 America Ground was under the sea and Robertson Street did not exist![9]

However, it does take its name from a notorious, eighteenth-century Hastings smuggler called John French, who was very active until he was arrested in his bed by customs officers and removed to Hastings prison. John French was one of the original squatters of America Ground and the mural painted on the adjacent wall in 2001 shows a typical scene of America Ground from the early nineteenth century.

French's Bar, the first pub to open in Robertson Street, is now surrounded by many other licensed premises. It is a free house popular with Hastings youth.

Hare and Hounds
Old London Road, Ore

The Hare and Hounds is known to have existed in 1777, but was probably much older. It has a special niche in local history because the town's first theatre, a small playhouse built in 1806, was attached to the pub, situated at that time just outside the town boundary.[1] It was located here because theatre was thought to be a corrupting influence on the working classes and was not allowed in Hastings itself.

The Hare and Hounds was five minutes walk from Halton Barracks, built in 1804, where troops were stationed in readiness for the threatened invasion by Napoleon. The troops were good customers of the Hare and Hounds and on 1st July 1806 the first performance of a comedy called *The Soldier's Daughter* was shown here. But by 1809, when the garrison was reduced, the audiences dwindled and the theatre was forced, at times, to put on shows of performing dogs.[2]

The Shakespearean actor Edmund Keane, on a visit to Hastings a few years later, offered to play Shylock in the *Merchant of Venice* for one night only. He was accompanied by R.W. Elliston, a leading comedian of the day, and the evening was a resounding success.[3] The scenery painter, Thomas Sydney Cooper, who worked in the theatre for a short period, described how the two actors gave a most hilarious lunch to the company. Another tragic piece performed here was based on a murder at a local beauty spot and was written by a local historian.

The pub was considerably enlarged in 1810 with several bedrooms, stables for eight horses, one and a half acres of meadow and a fenced tea garden but in 1868 a fire destroyed both the inn and the theatre. A new public house was built on Old London Road, a little to the south-west of the old inn, which was in the area now known as Saxon Road. The theatre is remembered on an inscribed tablet on a nearby wall, unveiled by Sir Herbert Beerbohm-Tree, a famous Edwardian actor-manager, in 1914.

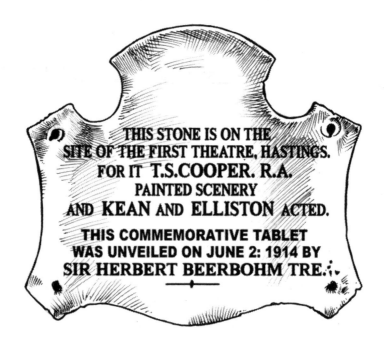

THIS STONE IS ON THE SITE OF THE FIRST THEATRE, HASTINGS. FOR IT T.S.COOPER. R.A. PAINTED SCENERY AND KEAN AND ELLISTON ACTED.

THIS COMMEMORATIVE TABLET WAS UNVEILED ON JUNE 2: 1914 BY SIR HERBERT BEERBOHM TRE...

By the early 1900s the Hare and Hounds registered 410 members of the Equitable Friendly Society, which provided insurance against sickness, old age and death. The membership comprised 300 men, twenty women and ninety juveniles. Because the juvenile members were not allowed into the pub, the society had its own entrance to a large upstairs room, where they met and sat down to 'beef pudding and plum suppers'.[4] The branch may have moved to the Clive Vale Hotel a few years later.

During the First World War, the pub was revisited by the military, this time by Canadian soldiers, 7,000 of whom were billeted in the town. The landlord hinted at the headache of their custom in 1918 when he transferred to the Cricketers, which he said, 'was a much easier house to manage than the Hare and Hounds'.

The pub was also the home of a tontine club, a type of Friendly Society, which shared out its funds at the end of each year. The tontine operated for several years and was run by secretary Isaac Pattenden. He collected members' weekly subs, kept an account and handed the total to the landlord. The money was then banked with the brewers, who took charge of it as an investment until the end of the year. Any remaining savings that accumulated were 'scooped' by the last living member.

Just before Christmas 1933, it was found that the landlord had absconded with £50 8s [£50.40] of the tontine funds. Tamplin's the brewers made good the deficit, remarking that at the time there were a lot of poor people in the district of Ore and they 'wanted to stand by them'. The landlord, James Pritchard, was committed for trial for fraud and given three months imprisonment.[5] The only other known tontine club in the town operated out of the Marina Inn in Caves Road.

For many years the Hare and Hounds ran popular darts and shovepenny teams. It fielded teams in the Hastings league and in the brewery league, but in the 1960s at least, the landlord and landlady organised their own championships and awards. Annual winners had their names inscribed onto silver trophies for darts and for shovepenny. In 1965 they added a third trophy, for cribbage.

This old pub closed in 2006. It had been an integral part of the Ore community for at least two and a half centuries. It is now awaiting redevelopment.

Hastings Arms
George Street, Old Town

The Hastings Arms dates from at least 1794, when it was described as 'a commercial inn of good reputation',[1] serving the military personnel billeted in Hastings, waiting for Napoleon.

In 1814, to celebrate the end of the war, the pub erected a sign described as 'an illuminated transparency, exhibited to represent the genius of Britain at whose feet lay in abject despair the fallen Corsican hero, with cherubs ascending to proclaim peace'.[2]

From 1827 to 1840, Richard Harman, previously a tailor, was landlord. He came to fame after a court case in which he sued the local Tory MP, Joseph Planta, to recover £24 6s 6d [£24.32] spent in the general election of 1837. In 1832 Planta had opposed the Reform Bill, which gave the vote to certain groups of men for the first time. Consequently he was not re-elected. He stood again in 1837 and engaged Harman, 'well versed in electioneering tactics' and a reform supporter, as his agent. Planta knew he had little chance without Harman's support but Harman agreed to act for him if he agreed not to attempt to alter the Reform Act.

Planta agreed but many voters were suspicious. However, corruption was rife and many 'pink voters' were bribed. 'Pink voters' were men who voted Conservative but wanted an extension of the franchise (i.e. wanted the vote to be given to more people). Planta gave several Hastings pubs 'carte blanche' to treat potential voters with free drink. The Horse and Groom, the Hastings Arms, the Sussex Tap, the King's Head and many others across town were involved in this corruption.

In court, evidence was produced to show that several public houses had received cash for treating customers who had the vote. More funds were distributed to tradesmen and artisan voters who were supporters of reform and their wives were treated to tea and sugar. Harman won the case and was granted £15.[3]

During this period, the rear of the pub was known as the Hastings Arms Shades, suggesting that prostitutes used the back of the premises.[4] It was also socially acceptable for customers to snatch some sleep in the small back bar. A fisherman, for example, could call in after a trip, take some beer and have a nap. In 1851, James Noakes, a higgler (hawker), is recorded sleeping with his head on his lap. Similar occurrences are recorded in the Queen Adelaide (three doors away) and also in the Cutter.[5]

One evening during the First World War, five Canadian soldiers in the same bar were drinking Canadian Red Seal Whisky. Although the landlord claimed they couldn't possibly be drunk on the amount he had sold them, they nevertheless appeared to be. In court they claimed they had been doped and that their drinks had been spiked with 'snow', otherwise cocaine, which must have been one of the first drug cases in the town. The chief constable claimed 'the whole Hastings police force were trained in the use of cocaine' and that the soldiers had perjured themselves. The landlord was fined £5 for permitting drunkenness.[6]

In the 1920s it was noted that the Hastings Arms income was poor in winter but excellent in summer. It was now a summertime bed and breakfast establishment, making a profit of around £200 a year and its summer visitors were now arriving by the latest mode of transport, the car.[7] The door panel on the left still reads 'Hotel Entrance'.

In 1961 an old hiding place for contraband spirits was discovered underneath two windowsills in a bedroom on the first floor. One contained four flasks each three feet deep. The second sill contained another three flasks and all were connected to the bar by metal pipes. Each flask was capable of holding eight gallons [36 litres] and they were estimated to be 200 years old. The first recorded licensee was Mrs Sargent, a widow, in 1794. However, there is an account of smugglers adjourning to Pip Sargent's after running a cargo, which suggests the house may have been licensed before that date.[8]

In the 1980s the pub was featured in the *Flook* strip cartoon by Hastings resident and jazz clarinetist Wally Fawkes, along with other Hastings landmarks, such as the pier.[9] The pub sign shows the town coat of arms, which should not be confused with the arms of the Cinque Ports towns.

Havelock
Robertson Street

The Havelock, originally a small town centre hotel was, after French's Bar, the second licensed premises in Robertson Street. It was first licensed in 1857[1] and by the 1870s it was doing a full trade, particularly in summer. On one occasion 180 children from the Licensed Victuallers' school in Kennington arrived by rail and marched to the beach 'to the merry strains of a well trained drum and fyfe band'. They went for a swim and a ramble and then marched back to the Havelock for dinner. They were accommodated at the Palace Hotel.[2]

Havelock Hotel, & Commercial House,

HAVELOCK ROAD,

AND

ROBERTSON ST., HASTINGS.

CHARLES DAVEY,

(Of London),

Having purchased the above Establishment, begs to inform the Inhabitants of the surrounding neighbourhood, and the Public generally, that he has laid in an entire fresh Stock of Old and Choice Foreign WINES and SPIRITS of the Finest Brands, and hopes by strict personal attention to business to receive an adequate share of support.

C. D. having had many years' experience in the trade, guarantees that all articles vended at this Establishment will be perfectly genuine, and not to be surpassed in quality or Price by any House in the trade.

All Malt Liquors from the most eminent Brewers.

Clean Measures kept expressly for Jugs.

1871

But not all the customers were as happy. In the same year an inquest was held into the suicide of a commercial traveller staying in the Havelock. The police found the deceased hanging by the neck with a long handkerchief tied to the bedrail. The waiter, Alfred Briggs, thought 'he had seemed vacant, lost and in low spirits'.[3]

In the early 1880s, just before the licence changed hands, a group of musicians playing outside was found to be blocking the road with a crowd nine feet [2.74m] deep. They told the constable that the landlord, who was about to transfer, had requested them to play a parting tune for him.

Perhaps he read the 'writing on the wall', as from now on circumstances began to change and with the onset of the economic depression, the Havelock began to suffer. In 1883 there was a reduction in profits, debts, a court summons and writs. Liquidation followed, the hotel closed and the Havelock became a simple pub.[4] At that time a passageway ran through the pub and was used by the public.

An interview in the book *Hastings at War*, mentions the Havelock passage in wartime: 'There was a god almighty explosion and we went into the passage of the Havelock pub, and we dived into that passage and threw ourselves onto the ground and lay there looking out. Along by Woolworths, a car was sent up into the air by the bomb and rolled over and over ... While we lay there, there was another terrific explosion down by Plummer's and I'll never forget seeing a huge lump of yellow coloured masonry come over and land on the tram wires ... I saw the wires stretch down and then up and back it went. I never knew where it went to, but it was a huge lump of masonry. When it had quietened down … this Canadian soldier came running over covered in blood and dirt. He picked up his motorbike which was lying on its side in the gutter, and dashed off towards Bexhill, about 80 miles an hour.'[5]

Cyril Pelluet recalls the Havelock in the late 1950s and another motorbike, under more pleasant conditions. 'The Havelock's attraction, at the time', he said, 'was the landlady's daughter. She was a star attraction, quite well built and she rode a 350cc motorbike. We all fancied her something rotten but none of us ever got anywhere.'[6]

Forty years later the Havelock came to national attention, when it was suddenly realised that its wall tiles were possibly Royal Doulton. The tiled walls in question include four separate pictures, each covering approximately half a wall, from floor to ceiling.

One shows General Havelock sitting astride a white horse in uniform. Another is titled 'The battle of Hastings A.D. 1066'. A third shows the ruins of Hastings Castle and a fourth, a sea battle between three vessels. Of the three vessels, two are named. One is *Conqueror* which bears the port registration 'Hastings' and the other is a French ship *Le Cormoran Affamé* (The Hungry Cormorant). Local folklore states that the timber from the French vessel is the timber seen today forming the ceiling of the Havelock's ground floor bar.

It seems unlikely that the artist would have named the ships and depicted a battle in such a large picture with so much detail and presumably considerable cost, if the event was entirely fictional. The

General Havelock

Royal Doulton Museum has suggested that the pictures date from between 1890 and 1917, although during alterations to the Royal Albion in 1911, the landlord said he would 'like pictures on the wall like the Havelock'. The pub was immediately listed Grade II.[7]

In the 1980s the Havelock was renamed the Cask and Kettle and became a managed Phoenix pub. In 1984 it put on pensioners' mornings, with free newspapers and 20p off every pint. Other Phoenix pubs in the town complained to the brewery and got the same reduction. The new name lasted for a few years, but eventually reverted back to the Havelock in 1995.

Hole in the Wall and the Kicking Donkey
Hill Street, Old Town

The Hole in the Wall and its sister pub the Kicking Donkey were located opposite each other in Hill Street. The Ole in the Wall started selling beer in 1858,[1] when it was a grocery shop with an on licence. The first landlord was John Heathfield, who transferred from the Kicking Donkey. The business gradually transformed into a simple beer house, a status it kept until 1952.

In 1926 magistrates considered closing both pubs on the grounds of redundancy,[2] which was a contradiction, as the police admitted there were more customers in the Ole in the Wall when they visited than in any other pub in the Old Town. The police described the pub as 'cramped and unsuitable' and objected to the poor lighting of the bar and to a small passage alongside which led to alleys and small cottages to the rear. The brewers purchased the cottage next door for enlargement of the premises, but in the same year the building suffered a severe fire. After renewal a more modern, larger pub appeared.

A popular landlord was William Smith who arrived in Hastings in 1912. From 1918 to 1931 he worked on the railways and then in 1931 he became licensee of the Ole in the Wall, which was described at the time as having a 'dark atmosphere'. It seems the enlargement had not improved the lighting. Nevertheless it was obviously a good business, selling 400 barrels a year and producing £300 annual profits. Smith died in 1937,[3] just before the pub found brief fame by reaching the final in the *Observer* Darts Tournament in 1938.

Many supporters accompanied the darts team to the Cambridge clubroom to watch the semi-final between the Ole in the Wall and the Victoria, Hollington and again the following week for the final with the Lord Nelson in the Market Hall, George Street. Admission to the final was by ticket only and by all accounts this was a major event with 'yells of jubilation and groans of disappointment from an excited crowd of 400 spectators'. The Ole in the Wall team was only just beaten, even though three of its players were under twenty and were not so experienced.

Fifty-four pubs entered the tournament with 110 teams and 1,000 players but both the finalists were from the Old Town, which suggested they 'had the best players' [cheers and boos]. The team had obviously much improved since 1935 when they entered the Watney's Darts

Competition with fourteen other pubs, but were knocked out early in the competition.[4]

Two regulars in 1944 were Bert Thomas and Charlie Thomset, who were both posted abroad with the Hastings Company of the Royal Sussex Regiment. Early that year Bert had the bad luck to lose his left foot to a German mine and was shipped home. 'Job for you laddy', he said to Charlie on leaving, 'find that foot, pickle it and fetch it home'.

Some months later Charlie arrived home on leave and found Bert in the 'Ole in the Wall, in position at the head of the bar. 'Where's my foot?' he said and Charlie had to tell him he didn't have it. 'That's it, bloody typical. Give you a simple job and you let me down'. 'Sorry Bert', said Charlie, 'but you can't get the vinegar, y'know'.[5]

In 1952, the licence of the George, All Saints Street, which had recently closed, was transferred to the Hole in the Wall and the pub finally became fully licensed.[6] Ron and Rose French ran it from 1957 for its final fourteen years, before moving to the Jenny Lind in 1971. Its sign showed a fist holding a bottle of beer through a hole in a brick wall.[7] The name is misleading as the pub was situated some distance from the site of the old Hastings town wall. A second Hole in the Wall existed in Claremont in the 1860s.

The Kicking Donkey is listed as a beer house in the 1855 directory when the licensee was John Heathfield,[8] although the building is much older. It was inherited by Mary Glyde in the 1860s and from 1894 was known as the Seagull, a most suitable name for a Hastings pub, before reverting back to the Kicking Donkey in 1899. In 1923 it changed its status from a simple beer house to a fully licensed public house. In 1926 it was declared redundant by the chief constable, but was reprieved.

In 1936 it was granted a licence for bar billiards, a game then coming into vogue, providing it was not played on Sundays, Christmas Day or Good Friday.[9] On these days the landlord was required to dismantle the billiard table and store it in a cupboard so as not to offend St Clement's Church at the end of the street. The Kicking Donkey was one of the first Hastings pubs to promote the game of bar billiards, which started in England in the 1930s and was developed from the traditional game of bagatelle. Sussex in particular was — and is — a hot bed of bar billiards activity.

In 1947 the Kicking Donkey became licensed to sell wine[10] but nine years later, in 1956, it was declared redundant a second time and was closed. Its history as a former pub made it a desirable residence and in 1995 it was sold for £97,000.

The story goes that the name Hole in the Wall originates from the Kicking Donkey. The donkey kicked a hole in the wall when it realised there was another pub nearby. A second tale relates that King George once visited the house but was too large to get in so they knocked a hole in the wall for him.

Both premises proudly display their history. Above the original doorway a bas-relief of a kicking donkey recalls this pub of the past, while the private house opposite has kept the name Hole in the Wall.

Horse & Groom
Mercatoria

The Horse and Groom was built in 1829 by glazier Stephen Millsted for the benefit of the workforce busy constructing the new town of St Leonards. It is on record that they were so thirsty that the pub opened before the windows were installed.[1]

Workers also came to the Horse and Groom on Saturday nights to be paid their wages and were called in from the street one by one They came again on Sundays to quench another thirst, this time to listen to the newspapers being read aloud. Edward Thebay was 'Sunday reader' at the Horse and Groom for many years.[2]

The Horse and Groom was regarded as a 'Tory rendezvous' and in the parliamentary election of 1835, the Conservative candidate William Planta, had one of his committee rooms here. It was common practice to bribe the voters and the Horse and Groom gave out a butt of porter plus wine, spirits and ale every day of the campaign in support of the corrupt Tory candidate (see the Hastings Arms).[3]

Among the staff who worked here were Mrs Raven the cook, and a potboy called George. A story was told that one day in 1834 George complained about Mrs Raven's beef puddings with suet in the crust. 'I really can't eat it missus', he said. 'Well, if you promise not to tell that I make my puddings without suet, I will see what I can do'. Afterwards George in blissful ignorance of the fact that the only difference from before was that the suet was chopped smaller said he had 'never tasted a better pudding'.[4]

An early landlord, John Woods, was described as cheerful, with a simple integrity and a strict disposition, but ill fitted to be a publican. For sport or for gain his customers, after taking a drink from their pots, would shout: 'Look here Woods, do you call this a proper measure?' He refilled their pots, not realising he had been duped. After a year he gave up to become Hastings's postmaster.[5]

In 1860 a case dubbed 'Goodbye Brother Chip' filled the local court. One evening three friends, two of them carpenters, called into the passage alongside the private bar for pots of ale. At the end of the evening one said to the other: 'Good night brother chip'. The reply he received was, 'I shan't shake hands with you. I am a master' implying he was a superior, better carpenter. A scuffle started and one man fell to the ground and lost consciousness. By morning he was pronounced dead from concussion. The court decided it was a case of manslaughter and it was referred to Lewes Assizes.[6]

'Lost' pubs around Mercatoria include the Anchor, East Ascent (1830s–1905), the Coach and Horses, Mews Road (1846–1950), the British Hotel, now Clarence House, opposite the Horse and Groom (1833–1906), the White Hart, Norman Road (1856–1953), the New

Inn, Mercatoria (1830s–1869) and the Star in the West, Undercliffe (1852–1943).

In 1871 they were threatened by the London matchbox trick. A tramp who called in for a drink was accused of stealing a bottle of whisky. He took a light for his clay pipe from the gas lamp behind the bar and turned out the lamp. Whilst the barman searched for matches the tramp snatched a bottle of whisky. In court he claimed he had never heard of of the matchbox trick, had never been to London and had walked straight from Edinburgh. He got three months.

During the First World War, many Canadian soldiers were customers. Mary Dann, who lived in Harold Mews, was charged with 'supplying intoxicants to soldiers, with intent to make them less efficient'. She had purchased a considerable amount of beer and spirits in the Horse and Groom and seven Canadians were found drunk in her house. She received a brutal three months imprisonment.

A few months later, landlord Ernest Tompkins was charged under the same Defence of the Realm Act, but this time three witnesses gave contradictory evidence and the case was dismissed. His lawyer remarked: 'If this man is found guilty no pub in England is safe'.[7]

In 1985 the Victorian windows were replaced and became the subject of a complaint by a local amenity society. Without planning permission, for the pub is listed, the landlord removed Stephen Milstead's original windows and replaced them with multi-panelled, imitation Regency ones.[8]

In 1999 the Horse and Groom had another brief moment of fame, when one of its customers hit the national headlines. Regulars were dumbfounded when they read in the national press that fellow drinker Alan Kelly, of Norman Road, had turned up in Serbia among a group of Kosovan freedom fighters being disarmed by NATO troops. Frustrated by the atrocities he had seen on television at home in St Leonards, he had volunteered for two months.

Landlord David Sansbury said: 'He told us he was going to Kosovo and everybody in the pub chuckled and wondered how far he would get. Anyone who can help the Kosovars in any way is doing good, but you would hardly call him a prize-fighter and I have not heard that he has had any military experience.' He added: 'I defy you to dislike him. He is a bloke who likes a drink, real ale is his tipple.'[9]

This pub was listed in the *Good Beer Guide* between 1999 and 2009.

Jenny Lind
High Street, Old Town

The Jenny Lind opened around 1850[1] on the site of the Bell, a pub that
dated back to at least 1613. The Jenny Lind was a free house until
1898, when Watney's purchased the freehold.

Before the First World War, the chief constable threatened to
close down the pub because 'it was not being conducted to his
satisfaction'. However, not enough money could be found for the
compensation payment and the pub was reprieved.

During the war landlord James Smith was convicted for serving out of hours. In 1918 he was convicted a second time, for serving a lance corporal at 4pm, an offence under the wartime regulations. When the constable who saw this entered the pub, Smith attempted to bribe him. For this he was heavily fined and lost his licence. After an agreement was made between the brewers and the magistrates, the landlord was replaced.[2]

In 1932 the police opposed the Jenny Lind licence a third time, because of 'poor sanitation'. Watney's agreed to make improvements and acquired an adjacent house that allowed them to enlarge the pub to the size it is today. The Jenny Lind was reprieved once again.

During these improvements some old woodwork belonging to St Clement's Church was discovered embedded in the walls. A spokesman for the church said: 'The various pieces of oak formed part of the ancient rood screen of the church, which was probably taken down during the Commonwealth. The larger pieces can still be seen in the roof of the south aisle, where they were used to repair the damage caused by the attack of a hostile fleet in 1652. The smaller pieces were for the most part destroyed, but some were preserved by being built into the wall of a house facing the north-east corner of the church. The main beam that spanned an aisle or the nave, the lintel of the central arch, three pieces of arcading and several uprights, were discovered; and the smaller pieces were handed over to the Parochial Church Council for preservation by the owners of the house.'[3]

On the outbreak of the Second World War and with the evacuation of the town during the Battle of Britain, the Jenny Lind closed and in 1941 its licence was transferred to the brewers.[4] In 1943 it was badly bombed and after the war it was completely rebuilt. The old interior of the back bar was restored with old timbers and the pub re-opened in 1951.[5]

In 1957 the licence was granted to the British light-heavyweight boxing champion, Don Cockell, remembered for his famous fight with Rocky Marciano for the world title in 1955. However, he didn't stay long and in May 1959 he gave up the licence.[6]

In 1980 landlord Graham Browne had to argue to get his licence. He had previously been the licensee of Tumbledown Dicks in Farnborough, described as 'one of the toughest pubs in

_HR_

OPEN MIKE
AT
THE JENNY

First Session: Thursday 26th October at 8pm

Featuring
John Hendrickse

Sessions held every Thursday
(poets & performers 7.30pm)

Come and read, play or perform

**Bring your own or your favourite poems,
songs or act to our Open Mike Sessions at:**
The Jenny Lind, High Street, Hastings Old Town

For further details see local press or telephone 01424 420879

1994

Britain and a favourite of military personnel returning from overseas duty. But by 1982 he was struggling. 'There are too many pubs in this small area', he said. 'I would close down if I could get a satisfactory settlement. We have lost money this year.'[7] But within ten years the local economy had improved and with it the Jenny Lind's fortunes.

In August 1990 the pub changed its name to the Penny Farthing, a name which lasted only a few months.[8] The pub was taken over by the Kingston Inn Co. in 1993.

Royalty apart, there are few women in pub names, but the Jenny Lind is an exception. Jenny Lind was a famous Victorian soprano known as the Swedish Nightingale and a hugely successful singer in Europe and America in the mid-nineteenth century. The gold rush town of 'Jenny Lind', California, is named after her and she is commemorated on the fifty krona Swedish bank note.

In recent years there have been attempts to prove she was a resident of Hastings. A previous landlord claimed she spent her retirement in Ore. There has been a suggestion that she lived in Bohemia and sang in St Clement's Church. Unfortunately there is no historical evidence to back up any of these claims, as yet. The pub sign is the only sign in Hastings made of stained glass and matches a stained glass window on the staircase.

Jolly Fisherman
East Parade

The Jolly Fisherman was first licensed to James Mann in 1834[1] and was located in front of the Stade, three doors from the London Trader beer house. In the 1850s the pub had an active cricket team, known as the Jollies, whose matches were reported in the local press. A typical match was played in 1854 between 'fishermen and mechanics' on the West Hill. The Jollies won this particular match by 109 runs to 29 and 118 runs to 65. It was the custom for both teams to celebrate afterwards in the pub.[2]

The following year, landlord Robert Swain was charged with 'disturbing the peace'. A police inspector claimed a fracas had developed when he asked him to close at 12.20am, ending in Swain's arrest. Swain was able to call several witnesses in his defence, who all said that the inspector was drunk and 'had some little ill feeling towards the Jolly Fisherman and its landlord'. Swain claimed he was outside the pub only 'to see if the brig was ashore'. The magistrate refused to accept that the inspector was drunk but agreed he 'had exceeded his duties and had acted harshly, hastily and intemperately'. When the case was dismissed, the court, 'which was crowded with fishermen, found the decision to their great satisfaction.'[3]

In the same year, a woman was charged with being drunk and disturbing the peace at 3am. She claimed she and her friends had just left the Jolly Fisherman 'in consequence of a collier being ashore', which demonstrates that the Jolly Fisherman opened and closed on demand during the night to serve boat crews when they landed,[4] even though it was against the law to open before 4am but not illegal to open for the crews of colliers, London traders and brigs (see page 156).

In 1883 a visitor to Hastings left a carpet bag in the third class waiting room at Hastings station. He returned to find it missing. The thief gave the bag to the landlady of the Jolly Fisherman for safe keeping! It contained a nightshirt, slippers, a scotch cap, a flannel shirt, cigar case, flask, kid gloves, neck cloth and hairbrush. A fisherman in the bar bought the slippers for 6d [2½p] and the hairbrush for 2d. The thief was finally caught in a nearby beer house, the Free Trader, near the fish market, trying to sell the remaining items. When he was arrested he was wearing the flannel shirt and the neck cloth. He was charged and imprisoned for one month.[5]

Jack Hart, a fisherman interviewed by Steve Peak in the 1980s, said: 'Before the 1914–1918 war all the pubs used to open at 5am. There used to be more fights before 8am than there is all week now. There were often fights with the Ramsgate men (off the smacks working in Rye bay) out in front of the Jolly Fisherman. This was the most popular pub with fishermen because it was right in front of the fish market.'[6]

Pub opening hours were further controlled from 1869, so when the fish market was built in 1870, the pubs around it were granted 5am licences. The Jolly Fisherman got its early morning licence in 1875 but subsequently lost it, probably because of the decline of the fishing industry from 1900. When pub opening hours were further restricted during the First World War, the Jolly Fisherman tried to get its early licence back, but was refused.[7]

In 1925 it again applied for an early licence from 6.30am to 8.30am, on the basis that 'several hundreds of people are out and about at the fish market during these hours' and if the pub wasn't open 'fishermen wouldn't get their glass of milk and whisky'. The landlord said there were thirty big boats, forty-five small boats and in addition, fishermen from Rye on steam trawlers put into the harbour. But again the application was turned down.[8]

In 1942 the Jolly Fisherman, being on the front line, suffered from enemy bombs although it was not directly hit. When the nearby Prince Albert public house closed in 1954 Hastings Winkle Club moved into the Jolly Fisherman. Landlord Brian Hone became Winkle Club Treasurer until 1959.

In 1959 the licensee of the London Trader, then a beer house a few doors away and still trading today, applied for the transfer of the Jolly Fisherman licence. The application was successful and the Jolly Fisherman closed down. In the application the landlord of the London Trader pointed out that half his customers were fishermen. In reply the magistrates' clerk said, 'If the application is granted, they will all be jolly fishermen'. The transfer was granted.[9]

Today the building is a tiny restaurant called Foyles Tea Room, named after the TV series *Foyles War* which was filmed in Hastings. Its original two small bars now form one room. A small reminder of its colourful past can be seen in the name 'Jolly Fisherman' etched on the front window.

Laila
Havelock Road

This pub was first licensed in 1857 as the Old Golden Cross. It was then a much smaller building than the present one.[1] In 1867 the landlord applied for a licence for another premises at 53 Havelock Road, to be called the New Golden Cross, which was granted.[2] The Old Golden Cross was extended in 1890, when the house next door was purchased.[3] The two premises were completely rebuilt in 1899 and taken over by A.J. Jones, formerly a draper at Whiteley's. At the turn of the last century this new pub was, with one or two exceptions, considered the best that Hastings had to offer; a fine artistic building in Renaissance style. The following description paraphrases a report from that time.[4]

Its chief feature, apart from the cupola with the resplendent cross on top, was a series of handsome columns which outlined the windows. The rooms on the first floor comprised a billiard room, a lodge room and a reception room. The billiard room was well lit and magnificently decorated with a heavy embossed wallpaper having a large and beautiful chrysanthemum design. The room was fitted all round with rich leather and dark wood lounge seats. The final touch was a high and graceful fireplace, which occupied one end of the room and completed the harmony with the rest of the furniture.

The billiard room ceiling was panelled in plaster relief that extended down onto a frieze of considerable depth, whose pattern was partly based on the chrysanthemum wallpaper. All the upholstery and furnishing was the work of Maple's of Tottenham Court Road. It was a room where the locals came not only to play billiards but also to admire and experience some luxury.

Next to the billiard room was the lodge room, fitted for the use of secret societies, dazzling with the symbolism of the Druids, the Freemasons and the Buffaloes. At its far end, in front of a projecting carved window, was a curtain dais where the druid's throne was located. Decorated pedestals, appropriate to the druidical ceremonies, were prominent. The lodge room was furnished with long mahogany tables and handsomely decorated chairs.

From the first floor a grand staircase came down to the ground floor. At the foot it separated, one side to the main entrance, the other to the saloon bar. The ground floor was divided by handsome dark wooden partitions into four sections. The public bar, the plainest of the four, was a model of comfort with substantial wooden benches of a perforated design.

Similar to the description of the Cricketers given by Robert Tressell, there were also two private bars. The saloon bar was a luxurious lounge of sofas and easy chairs upholstered in Moroccan leather. It contained some handsome tapestry work designed around historical subjects and framed in heavy plush velvet, which lent the room a dignity and comfortable appearance.

The report from which this description is taken described the barmaids as 'a bevy of damsels as dexterous and charming as ever was the celebrated Hebe, who waited on the assembled gods of Olympus, who, however delicious was the nectar they drank, certainly never took their refreshment in a maple fitted bar like that in the Old Golden Cross'.

The report mentions finally the electric lighting, pointing out the lamp brackets as a most striking feature, especially in the downstairs bars. The whole installation was carried out by the Southern Electrical Engineering Company on its free wiring system, 'and was a splendid example of the latest in art glass globes and art brackets'. Including the great sign that was originally out front, there were about two hundred lamps in the house, requiring no small amount of current when all were turned on at once. Spacious cellars and vaults completed the scheme of this palatial public house.

The Old Golden Cross closed during the Second World War and suffered severe blast damage from a bomb explosion on nearby buildings. In 1950 its sign was included in Whitbread's miniature inn signs series.[5] In the same year the brewers vandalised the building by ripping out all of the interior for use in a pub conversion in London. In 2003 it was renamed Hero's Venue Bar and redesigned as a teenage music venue. With the arrival of the University Centre opposite, it will no doubt stay that way. In 2008 it was renamed again, as Laila.

Lord Nelson
East Bourne Street

The Lord Nelson was built and first licensed in about 1830. Formerly the Nelson Inn, it stands just within the line of the Hastings old town wall, on a site that was originally two blocks of stables adjoining an old brandy house, dating back to 1590.[1]

Fifty years later the Lord Nelson was in the news prior to the general election of 1880. Steve Peak in his book *Fishermen of Hastings* says: 'In the 1880 general election, the Liberal Party lost one of its two Hastings MPs in a swing to the Conservatives and decided to retaliate by forming local associations.... The Fishermen's Liberal Association was founded at a meeting in the Lord Nelson pub on 17th April, 1880, when 100 fishermen heard a rallying speech... by Thomas Brassey MP. The Liberals had been criticised of being out of touch with fishermen's issues, particularly on the question of the loss of beach.'[2]

Interestingly enough, in 1882, the *Hastings and St Leonards News* believed that the fishing community was somehow cut off from the town and that 'the want of wider social sympathies impels fishermen to congregate in public houses' like the Lord Nelson.[3]

In 1904 the Nelson closed for several months and a notice in the window advertised the pub to let at £24 per year. No one was prepared to rent it, which gave the police reason to claim it was redundant and should close. However, the year before it had been sold by the brewery and was now a free house. The new owner bought the house anticipating the restrictions of the new Licensing Act of 1904, which allowed pubs tied to breweries to be closed on the grounds of redundancy, even though they might have a good record.[4]

The police tried to close it again in 1911. This time they were complaining about the difficulty of supervising the back doors. But in court popular landlord Harry Haste was praised for the good conduct of the pub and, among other things, the 'well attended sing-songs'. 'You'll make me blush, if you carry on talking like this', he said. Nevertheless the chief constable still claimed that the Nelson was redundant and should close. Finally, it was decided that the licensee of a free house could not be awarded compensation out of brewery funds and, as the house was not tied to a brewery, the case was dropped.[5]

For the next twenty-seven years little is heard about the Lord Nelson until, in 1938, its darts team won the *Observer* Annual

Darts Tournament. Fifty-four pubs entered the competition with 110 teams and over 1,000 players. The final, between the Hole in the Wall and the Lord Nelson, both Old Town pubs, was held in the Market Hall, George Street and was attended by 400 paying spectators. The team captains thanked the players for their sportsmanship and both teams went to the Nelson for a drink out of the cup.[6]

In the 1960s new drinking companions joined the local fishermen. In 1967 a barman, who was also a folk singer, received a hefty prison sentence of fifteen months for selling cannabis to German language students who used the bar during the summer. At this time it had a reputation as a 'trouble spot'.[7]

Peter Skinner was a regular at the time: 'When we were young and very drunk', he says, 'we used the Lord Nelson, which was a wild pub. If it was the same today they'd close it down. There was a lot of folk singing, a lot of villainous characters and it was very exciting when you were drunk.' And with an echo from 1882 (see above), Peter said 'a lot of fishermen drank there. They didn't really mix with other groups in the town — always a group unto themselves.'[8]

Another regular in the mid 1970s was Mick Nurse. He recalls that the Nelson was popular with bikers at the time and had the best jukebox in Hastings. On a return visit twenty years later nothing much had changed.[9]

In 1982 there was a brief return to the days of the early morning licence, when the Nelson got permission to open at 5am to serve local fishermen returning from a night's fishing.[10] In 1988 the Nelson Tigers Social Club (formed in 1977 to play rugby) staged the first of several open-air rock concerts on the Stade. Many thousands of pounds were raised for the Hastings lifeboat and by 1994 it had become the town's 'premier annual gig'.[11]

By the 1990s Old Town artists had adopted the Nelson and in 1991 an art exhibition was held in the pub which, surprisingly, sold £1,500 worth of pictures, prompting the landlord to hold monthly exhibitions.

Marina Fountain

Caves Road, St Leonards

The Marina Fountain stands at the western boundary of Burton's St Leonards. Formerly the Fountain Inn, it was erected in about 1837[1] by Stanton Noakes, a blacksmith, on the banks of the River Asten, which then ran along the route of Grosvenor Crescent.[2] The river inspired Keats: —

> *So far her voice flowed on,*
> *like tumerous brook.*
> *That lingering along a pebbled coast*
> *Doth fear to meet the sea.[3]*

At that time, the area to the north was farmland and the pub served the needs of farmers and farm workers, many of whom resided in Caves Road.

The Fountain's trade was boosted in the 1840s when large numbers of railway navvies arrived to build the railway from West St Leonards to Hastings, and to dig out the tunnel in the cliffs behind. In January 1845 a dinner was held to celebrate the arrival of the railway and the opening of the new West St Leonards station. The 1851 census indicates the hard life of the landlord and landlady. Not only did they run the pub, they also had ten children and thirteen railway navvies as lodgers, with only one live-in servant.[4]

The cliffs behind the pub have often been a problem. In 1850 a horse belonging to a railway contractor fell over the cliff and was so badly injured it had to be put down.[5] In 1860 twenty tons [20,321kg] of earth and rock fell onto a stable at the back of the pub, tragically killing John Barker, a homeless man who was living there.[6] Some other customers actually lived in the cliffs. In the 1850s William Smith and family had a cave with all 'mod cons' including a stable, a kitchen and a chicken house.[7] For insurance reasons, the cliffs are now bricked over down to the level of the pub garden.

After the railway navvies came the hop pickers. In September 1864 the *Hastings News* reported that 'large numbers of Irish hop pickers' had arrived in the countryside around Hastings and were lodging at the pub. At the end of the season, some of them stayed on to work on the new drainage system being built for St Leonards.[8]

During the First World War the licence was transferred several times. In 1917 it was transferred to Ernest Underwood, formerly of the Bromley Arms, Bow. He took over the Fountain because it was a 'quiet neighbourhood', very different from the East End of London but he stayed only a few months.

The next landlord, Walter Emery, was charged with harbouring military goods. When the military police searched the pub they found two whole cheeses in a tub in a passage at the end of the bar, another 20lbs [9kg] of cheese on a shelf, 56lbs [25kg] of sugar, a large amount of cocoa, army blankets, three army sweaters and a Ross rifle among other things. Walter Emery was jailed and the Fountain closed down for a time,[9] until the licence was transferred yet again to Arthur Clementson, formerly of the Railway, St Leonards, who stayed until 1919. But he had a heart problem and the licence was transferred yet again to Mr and Mrs Susan. On the outbreak of the Second World War licensee J.S. Clee was much more patriotic, acting as an unpaid air raid warden for the area.

By the 1950s the Fountain was feeling the competition from television and, along with other pubs, it lobbied the magistrates for an extra half-hour. 'Customers with television stayed at home until ten, which didn't give them much time for a drink', said the landlord. The half-hour was refused.

Ten years later the successful Fountain Games and Social Club was refused an extension because it had not issued membership cards In 1964 the club team became the Watney's shovepenny champions In 1967 and 1968 they won both the shovepenny and darts shields and in 1968 one customer, R. Ranson, was East Sussex, *News of the World* darts champion.[10]

In 1996 the Fountain was renamed the Marina Fountain when the Marina Inn at the other end of Caves Road closed. Today the Marina Fountain is a bikers' pub, catering especially for disabled bikers. The bar is a shrine to the Harley Davidson with a magnificent example mounted on the wall.

Biker Trefor Holloway recalls: 'I've lived in Hastings for forty years and used all the pubs here in my time. I've been a biker for many years and the pub that I use now is the Marina Fountain in St Leonards. The Marina Fountain has been a bikers' pub since about 2002 and it is used by the patch clubs, the guys with badges on the back of their leathers, because it's the only genuine bikers' pub in the town.

In other pubs drinkers you might think are bikers, only dress that way. A lot of them don't even have bikes. We call them plastic superficial. I'll give you an example. Some years ago I worked in an abattoir and a character known as Mad Dog Dan asked me for a pair of cow horns to attach to his crash helmet. He and his mates would go drinking, wearing cow horns on their helmets and beer mats sewn into their jeans. But the point is they don't ride bikes, they are just people who like to dress up. Why? Because this is Hastings and we're all a bit mad.

Genuine bikers in the patch clubs, including the Chopper club and the Nomads among others, are regulars at the Fountain on music nights and at weekends when we drink beer. Other nights we go on ride-outs to places like Box Hill, Newhaven or Rye. The Six Bells at Chiddingly is a favourite ride-out. On these nights we only drink Coke. That's why it's expensive. They wouldn't make any money out of us otherwise.

On May Day when Hastings is full of bikers who come in on the Hastings run, my girl friend and I and other bikers, drink in the London Trader and the Cutter.'[11]

Moda

Queens Road

This building dates from the 1850s, when it was part of Queen's Buildings. In 1866 it was known as the 'Wine and Beer Stores,[1] formerly of George Street'. It was granted a spirit licence in the same year and became the London Stores and Oyster Luncheon Bar.[2] The term 'London stores' was nineteenth-century slang for 'London whores' and the term 'oyster' was slang for a part of the female anatomy, indicating that the premises were used by prostitutes.[3]

In one of several cases involving prostitutes, the landlord was charged with 'unlawfully and knowingly permitting and suffering divers persons of a notorious bad character to assemble in his house against the tenor of his licence', following a visit by the police. The police found what they described as a 'mare's nest' inside the pub, accompanied by 'a great noise, caused by female voices'. In his defence, the landlord said he was busy serving the employees of Manger's Menagerie, who were pulling down the tent on the cricket ground nearby, and did not notice the women in the bar. He was fined £1 and asked the magistrate how he should deal with men from the cricket ground when they came into the pub to meet women. The magistrate's sexist response was a typical example of the double standards of Victorian morality; he simply said the charge did not apply to men at all.[4]

The bar became the Central Hotel in 1875[5] and narrowly escaped demolition in the late 1870s to make way for the new town hall built next door in 1881.

In the 1880s the Central Hotel was the headquarters of the Borough Bonfire Boys Society, one of at least four bonfire societies in nineteenth century Hastings. Large numbers of bonfire boys (up to 120) held their suppers and meetings at the Central Hotel but by 1887 they had moved to the Red Lion in Stone Street. Henry Link, late landlord of the Central Hotel, was treasurer of the society for eight years and was awarded a 'Handsomely Framed Illuminated Address' by them in 1887.[6] The society was still based at the Red Lion in 1890.

From 1942 to 1945 the Central Hotel was used by American troops when on leave passes. The late Charles Banks, then Police Inspector Banks, remembered that: 'On the whole they were well behaved, but there were quarrels at times with Canadian and British troops, mainly caused by the high rates of American pay'.[7] In

VICTORIAN CORDIALS

Drinks on sale at the London Stores in the 1870s included spirits mixed with cordials. The cordials were made from cloves, mint, shrub, noyeau, raspberry, ginger and real Dantzic spruce, among others.

A cordial was an alcoholic infusion of herbs or other plants or parts of plants, often thought to have invigorating or stimulating properties. There are examples of Hastingers drinking various mixes of spirits and cordials usually in half pints. A half pint of 'gin and peppermint' was one favourite. Many of these drinks were served hot in the winter particularly to 'flys' i.e. the drivers of horse-drawn taxis.

Noyeau is of Dutch origin and made from the flowers of the hawthorn tree. When in full bloom the petals were bottled with quality French brandy and sealed. The mixture was then left to stand for three months before being strained off.

Shrub. The recipe for shrub is apparently a secret of the J.R. Phillips company of Bristol. They claim their shrub recipe has been handed down over the years and has a long West Country heritage. Shrub was originally used during the days of rum smuggling to disguise the bitter taste of sea water that might have got into the rum barrels during the perilous journey from ship to shore. The traditional drink for shrub is 'Rum and Shrub' but it can be drunk neat. Sometimes known as 'Old English shrub' it was 5.3% proof.

Dantzic spruce. (Gdańsk or) Dantzic spruce is probably better known as an ingredient in the well-known Polish spruce beer. In Victorian times 'Real Dantzic Spruce' was a popular cordial made from an essence of the green buds of the black spruce fir tree which were dissolved in a strong syrup to which yeast and spices were added.

December 1945 the pub was renamed once more to become the G.I.[8] commemorating the war time patronage of the pub by American troops. Before the war, the American military had been told that they would be welcome in British pubs, if they remembered that the pub, generally, was a working man's place, where men come to meet their friends, not strangers. But after the war, Norman Longmate, in his book *The GIs* said: 'The final proof that the pub, the most English of institutions had taken the American serviceman to its heart came, when the Central Hotel, Hastings was formerly renamed the G.I.'[9]

At the renaming ceremony, Sergeant William Hastings of Texas, who had married a bride from Hastings, unfurled a new pub sign. He was presented with a silver tankard and many local, county, army and US dignitaries made speeches. The name G.I. put the pub into the *Guinness Book of Records*, as the shortest pub name in the country and also into Whitbread's miniature inn signs series, published in the 1950s.

But this was not to be the pub's final name. In 1962 it changed once more, to New Central. Peter Skinner recalls it a few years later. 'Sometimes we drank there but it wasn't very popular. At that time there was no shopping centre. The town centre didn't have the social density it has now, all those shops didn't exist. The area was quieter. I remember it as old, Victorian and semi-empty. They didn't serve baked potatoes. Instead they had little warm cabinets with steak and kidney pies wrapped in cellophane, and pickled onions. It wasn't a fashionable pub.'[10]

In 1979 it became the Town Crier, and then in the 1990s this elegant Victorian pub was gutted and 'remodelled'. In 1996 it was renamed again as Pitcher's Sports Bar and Diner. Ray Goode, Hastings's town crier (also one time national champion) was presented with the old pub sign, which was a portrait of himself. More recently it became Bar Moda, its seventh name change in over 150 years. More recently still, it is simply Moda.

Nag's Head
Gensing Road

The Nag's Head is located just outside the old boundary wall of St Leonards. It opened as a beer house around 1835 brewing its own ale. But by 1850 it was being supplied by the local St Leonards Brewery in Shepherd Street. It was granted a full licence in 1853.[1]

In 1855 the pub and the cottage next door were sold and merged together.[2] With more space it became a popular lodging house with eight bedrooms. In 1862 two sailors and a German bird seller were among its lodgers. The bird seller, Henri Veller, had 169 canaries in a large cage that he kept in the public bar. One day whilst he was out, the sailors stole some of the canaries and hawked them around the St Leonards pubs. The landlady of the Norman Hotel bought one, a customer in the Coach and Horses bought two and others were sold in London Road. After being charged with theft, the sailors were jailed, but still claimed they 'found the birds flying around in the skittle alley'.[3]

TO BREWERS AND OTHERS.

Valuable FREEHOLD PROPERTY, in the Parish of St. Mary Magdalen.

MR. VOYSEY

Has received instructions from the Proprietor to Sell by Auction, at the SOUTH SAXON HOTEL, St. Leonards, on THURSDAY, September 13th, 1855, at Two for Three o'clock in the Afternoon, in one lot (unless an acceptable offer be made by Private Contract, of which due notice will be given),

A DESIRABLE FREE PUBLIC HOUSE, situate in Gensing Road, in the parish of St. Mary Magdalen, in the Borough of Hastings, and known as the NAG'S HEAD INN, together with the COTTAGE adjoining. The above premises are now let to Mr. THOMAS CHAMPION, as a yearly tenant, at the annual rent of £40.

The above contains, on the ground floor, a convenient and well-arranged bar and room adjoining, a parlour, tap-room, and kitchen; one-pair floor, a large club room, two bed rooms, and a water closet; on the two-pair floor, four bed rooms; and a roomy cellar under the bar and parlour. In the rear thereof is a commodious covered skittle alley.

The Cottage adjoining consists of a parlour, kitchen, wash-house, and two bed rooms; now let to Mr. CHARLES LEE, as a weekly tenant, at 4s. 6d. per week.

For further particulars, apply to Messrs. MARTIN, Solicitors, High street, Hastings; or to the Auctioneer, 4, Eversfield place, St. Leonards. Of the latter may be had cards to view, and the terms of Sale by Private Contract.

A few years later, three tramping tailors 'who had worked the same board in Tunbridge Wells', and who were now working in St Leonards, lodged here.[4] Other lodgers included a 'bath chair man', who hired out an early form of wheelchair on the seafront and of course the usual building workers.[5]

For many years the pub was a popular skittles venue and on one occasion the landlord was fined for allowing skittles to be played for beer, a form of gaming. His licence was renewed, but only after a caution.

In the 1880s the Nag's Head became the headquarters of the St Leonards Bonfire Boys (founded in 1854), although in some years they used other St Leonards pubs. Their annual dinners, held in the clubroom on the first floor, were well attended with patriotic and nationalist toasts to the navy, army and Royal Family.

Each fifth of November the bonfire procession started here, headed by the St Leonards Town Band and the society banner. A lot of people were involved. On a typical fifth of November parade they carried 400 torches and everyone wore a costume: hussars, lancers, admirals and colonels were followed by the 'guy', usually about sixteen feet tall, on a coal wagon. Then more costumes: Turks, Irishmen, Chinese, Japanese and Indians followed by an illustrated banner depicting the arrest of Guy Fawkes. The procession marched around all the principal streets of St Leonards before joining other processions in Hastings. Finally the guy was burnt on the beach, opposite the end of London Road.[6]

Twenty years later Robert Tressell and other building workers employed by Jarrett and Adams, who had a workshop in Alfred Street, drank here. These men were to become famous as the *Ragged Trousered Philanthropists* in the book of that name by Robert Tressell. In the summer their annual beanos were organised in and started from, the Nag's Head. In 1906, for example, they travelled by horse and trap to the John's Cross pub near Robertsbridge to play cricket.[7]

The controversial pub sign showing a woman's head in a muzzle is another example of a pub sign in the Whitbread collection of miniature inn signs issued in the 1950s. The reverse of the Nag's Head miniature says: 'The scold's bridle went out of fashion some time ago. According to men this was because of a shortage of good old-fashioned steel, but according to ladies, because its application was never really necessary. It is better to dwell in the wilderness than with a contentious and angry woman.' However, it is not generally known that the sign was designed by a woman, Violet Rutter.[8] In 1854 the sign of another pub, the Original Good Woman, near the fish market, portrayed a woman carrying her severed head under her arm, which created a lot of protest in the local press.

In the 1950s and 1960s the Nag's Head was renowned for its darts team. On one memorable evening the team played a local archery club. The archers brought their own 'dartboard', an archery target, and used bows and arrows! When Michael Rose tried the bow, one of the arrows disappeared into the passageway and got embedded in the windowsill. It is not recorded who won the match.[9] In 1967 the team was the outright winner of the Battle of Britain Darts Cup organised by the Hastings RAF Association. Denny Gower, later a world darts champion and landlord of the Warrior's Gate in the 1970s, was team captain.[10]

In 1989 the Nag's Head closed. An old customer, Bert Tuppenny, recalled that he had been drinking there since the late 1930s and that his mother had used the pub for ten years before that. However, after refurbishment it opened again in 1991.

Norman Arms
Norman Road

The original Norman Hotel opened in about 1840,[1] twenty-five years before the completion of Warrior Square. Its early custom came from the shopkeepers and tradesmen of the developing St Leonards, many of whom used the 'smoke room', where each had his own regular chair and pewter tankard.

At the time, pubs were divided into separate bars used by different social classes. A smoke room was usually the equivalent of a lounge bar but more dignified and upmarket. The Norman's smoke room attracted upper middle class customers from the surrounding large Victorian houses.

In 1855, after two bad summers, the Town Improvement Association held a meeting here. Its members discussed the question of 'Why should Hastings and St Leonards rank inferior to Brighton, when nature had done so much for Hastings, while art had done so little ... while art had done so much for Brighton, while nature had done so little?' They decided there were not enough amusements in St Leonards and a good music hall would do the trick.[2]

As Warrior Square developed, the Norman's public bar became the meeting place for the grooms, valets, coachmen and servants employed by Victorian families of the square, who used the services found in Western Road.

One customer at that time was William Barnett, who called in for a drink during Easter 1868. He was cautioned by the police for obstructing Western Road with his Punch and Judy show, which he operated on St Leonards beach. He was cautioned again for being drunk in charge of it, after some boys started chanting 'Punch is drunk, Punch is drunk'. He claimed he had earned a very lucrative '£10 in four days' on the beach.[3]

The Norman has always had competition. In 1905 the licensing magistrates considered whether they should re-license the beer house next door, known as the Warrior's Arms. They noted that the Norman was doing a good trade but that the customers of the Warrior's Arms were 'undesirables', 'loose and idle people who generally stand at street corners', and that the landlady had been victimised by one of them, whom she had prosecuted. The Warrior's Arms was closed down in 1905[4] and is now a coin and stamp collectors' shop.

During the First World War Warrior Square became an overseas drafting depot. The Women's Auxiliary Army Corps, founded in

1917, was billeted in the square and took over some of the properties including number 64, which it used as an orderly room. Female volunteers for military duty were issued with uniforms, vaccinated and drilled in front of the statue of Queen Victoria, before marching up the square to their mess hall. Off duty hours were sometimes spent in the Norman and for many of them this was their last experience of England before being sent to France, from which many never returned.[5] The first draft of WAACs left for France in August 1917, fifteen months before the war ended.

After the First World War, the Norman became the headquarters of the St Leonards Bowls and Quoits Club, which had at least two teams. This club was very active in the 1920s.[6] From 1925 until 1953 the landlord was Leonard Collinson (Colly). As vice president of Hastings & St Leonards Snooker League he provided a first-rate billiards room, used by many successful pub teams who entered the annual *Hastings Observer* Snooker Championships.

The old pub stood for ninety-eight years until it was demolished and rebuilt by Wilfred Shippham of Kent in 1938. During its rebuilding, the Norman stayed open and provided a minimal service A popular feature of the new pub was the teak panelled dining room locally renowned for its selection of cheeses.[7] In 1939 it was reported that a practical joker took a pony upstairs and tied it to Colly's bed! His response to this prank is not recorded.

In the Second World War the Norman, unlike some other local pubs, never closed, although it was bombed by the Luftwaffe.[8] The local population was depleted by evacuation and supplies of beer were at times very poor. The billiards saloon in particular stayed open throughout the war years, when it was much in demand by the military personnel billeted in the nearby Adelphi Hotel. Members of the Home Guard also used the pub for concerts and social evenings.

The Normando Jazz Club ran for a period in the 1990s and in 1995 the Norman closed for a short period after the joint licensee absconded, owing a large sum of money to the brewery. The previous sign simply said 'The Norman', underneath Watneys Red Barrel The pub sign of a Norman soldier dates from around 2000. It is made of fibreglass and according to one source its image was downloaded from the internet.

North Star
Clarence Road, Bohemia

The North Star was built in the late 1860s by Joseph Wisden, who had been a guard on the London, Brighton and South Coast Railway for eighteen years. He was granted a licence in 1870[1] but his time as landlord was not a smooth one.

In 1877 he tried to sue the barmaid. Mary Jane Bell came to the North Star from Belfast, recruited by a local employment agency at £18 a year. But after a few months she wanted to leave because: 'He has criticised everything I have done since I arrived'. Wisden sued her for the cost of her fare to England and other monies. He had apparently proposed marriage and bought her a hat but she had refused both.

She must have been a popular barmaid, as several customers turned up in court to support her. The case went against the landlord and he lost. Mary Jane Bell was awarded two guineas [£2.10] and Wisden was hissed as he left the courtroom. As a result, the North Star lost a number of customers and a good barmaid.[2]

In those early years the North Star was also a lodging house and in 1878 Wisden was charged for turning away two soldiers who had been posted to Hastings for training and who were seeking accommodation. The 'billeting question' was a grievance among local publicans, who were obliged to accommodate soldiers and their horses at the 'soldier's allowance', a low rate of 4d [1½p] a night. He was represented in court by Hewett's Brewery of St Leonards who said the pub was being altered and regretted the landlord had not found them alternative accommodation, but he was still fined 40s [£2].[3]

A letter to the *Hastings and St Leonards Observer* a few years later, signed 'Bohemian Ratepayer', complained of the 'hawkers and others of the pikey fraternity who congregate around the North Star Inn and the fair that takes place here with a general turmoil of rough music, roundabouts, shooting galleries, coconut throwing, brawling and shouting by a lot of worthless vagabonds'. ('Pikey' is a derogatory nineteenth century slang term for gypsy or traveller that is thought to have derived from the word turnpike. It is still in use today.)[4]

In the 1870s and 1880s the North Star was the headquarters of the Bohemia Bonfire Boys, one of four principal bonfire societies in Hastings. The Bohemia society was founded in about 1860 and on the fifth of November each year they marched around Bohemia and then into town to join the main procession, before returning to Bohemia to burn the guy. The processions started at the North Star and everyone wore fancy costume dressed up as navy, army, police, highwaymen, crusaders, clowns and demons. They were led by a brass band and the merriment went on until midnight. At the end of the century the tradition for bonfire faded. When it resurfaced after the Second World War, it did so at the Wishing Tree, Hollington.[5]

Several customers over the years have worked at the Buckshole Reservoir and for the Water Company. In the early 1900s the Hastings Waterworks Benefit Society held its annual dinners at the North Star. Water inspector Fred Lock praised the manager of the waterworks as 'a gentleman who treated his staff as gentlemen'. The manager responded saying: 'The day has passed when the term "local board stroke" (another derogatory name) was applied to council employees'. A musical programme followed.[6]

In 1939, a few months before the outbreak of war, the North Star found brief fame when its darts team came second in the Annual *Observer* Darts Tournament. Although it beat around fifty other pub teams, the Hastings British Legion narrowly beat it in the final. In 1940 the North Star entered two teams.[7]

In 1991 Watney's sued the landlord for non-payment of rent, a massive £17,000 a year and claimed he occupied the pub as a trespasser. In 1996 the North Star closed for two months for refurbishment and reopened as a free house. Divisions between the bars were removed to create one bar.

The pub sign at the time showed only the name North Star under the ubiquitous Red Barrel. It was replaced with a new sign depicting the North Star, an early steam locomotive built by George Stephenson for the Great Western Railway in the 1830s. At one point the engine was shipped to New Orleans, but the New Orleans Railway Company could not afford the asking price and the North Star was duly returned to England.

Old England
London Road, St Leonards

After the Saxon Hotel, on the corner of London Road and Grand Parade, was licensed in 1833, licences were granted to several other St Leonards public houses, including the Old England,[1] which was first licensed in about 1840.[2]

However, the coming of the railway and the opening of Gensing Station (now Warrior Square Station) in 1851 meant the original building, barely ten years old, had to be pulled down as it was blocking the construction of Gensing Station Road, now King's Road. The Old England was then rebuilt on its present site.[3]

In the 1850s the licensee was William Mantell Eldridge, who was also licensee, at various times, of the Swan, the Saxon Hotel and Shades and the St Leonards Arms. He was also proprietor of the St Leonards Brewery, that stood opposite the Old England.[4]

In the early years the Old England Tavern was a lodging house used by employees of the South Eastern Railway Company. One lodger, a luggage porter at the new station, was not the healthiest of men and one morning he started coughing and spitting blood. He was carried from the station to his room at the pub, where he died. The doctor who examined him said that his left lung was badly diseased with a cavity the size of an orange and a burst blood vessel.

In its early years the Old England Tavern opened at 5am. The 1869 Licensing Act changed opening hours and in 1872 the pub applied to continue opening from 5am, on the grounds that it was serving fifty local building workers with breakfast. The magistrate pointed out that they didn't need a licence to serve breakfast but they could not serve alcohol and the early licence was refused.[5]

Who paid for the drinks was often decided by gambling with dice, cards and spinning boards, a practice which the police considered illegal, although it was 'only for beer'.[6]

On an evening in 1894, a drunken 'colonial type' came in with a loaded pistol. After a beer he ran off down King's Road and sat in a doorway. He said to the policeman: 'It would serve the curs right if I shot them'. He had lived forty years in the British colonies, where he was obliged to carry a gun. A magistrate told him he 'must not think he was in the wilds of India or Ireland' when he was in St Leonards and he was told to leave the gun at home.[7]

A more famous customer was socialist firebrand and barrow boy Alf Cobb, who in 1907 had a small greengrocer's shop a few doors away, in Cross Street. In 1910 he was selling strawberries from his barrow, which was parked 'caterways' (a Kentish term for diagonal) across the entrance to Cross Street and was summoned for wilfully obstructing the street with his barrow. In court, he said he went into the pub and 'called for an order' after pulling his barrow up London Road. But he was well known to the police as a champion of local barrow boys and when he came out he was 'nicked'. In court he defended himself vigorously and the case was dismissed.[8]

Over the years the Old England has had a lot of competition. The South Street car park behind the pub was the site of the Prince Alfred, which closed in 1921. The Prince of Wales, at the bottom of Cross Street, is still trading. A third pub, the Bird in Hand, was situated at the other end of South Street. The Robin Hood, Warrior's Gate, Foresters, St Leonards Arms and the Admiral Benbow were on the opposite side of London Road — nine pubs within a few hundred metres of each other.

In 1939 the Old England was extended into the house behind it in Cross Street, forming the building we see today.

Drinking in the blackout during the miners' strike 1972

Old King John
Middle Road, Ore

The Old King John was a beer house in the 1850s. In 1870 the landlord, John Woodhurst, lost his licence because his house was 'insufficiently rated' and it closed down. He very quickly made some alterations and applied for a new licence, which was granted.[1]

Every year for the next ten years he applied with sincerity for a full licence but was always refused, although he had been landlord of the beer house for eighteen years.[2] Eventually the licence passed to his widow, who ran the house until 1883.

In 1878 a coroner's inquest was held in the pub into the death of a year-old baby. It was a sad case. The father was in Lewes prison and the mother, May Cornford, twenty-two years old, had been in an asylum for eighteen months and had 'not been able to take care of herself, much less the child' and had not been able to look after the baby properly.

The case attracted great interest in Ore, where the mother was well known. During the inquest, crowds of local people gathered in the street outside the Old King John waiting for news of the case and the verdict. May Cornford was found guilty of manslaughter and sent for trial at Lewes Assizes.[3]

Until the late nineteenth century, customers drank out of glazed earthenware beer pots. These were possibly Lustreware, a traditional Sussex pottery made from the plentiful Wealden clay, or much more likely, hop pots made by a pottery in Rye and known as Ryeware. Rye is on the border of Sussex and Kent and the Old King John is just off the Hastings–Rye road. Glazed earthenware beer pots were cheap to produce compared to pewter, which was ten times more expensive. They went out of use with the introduction of glassware in the early twentieth century.[4]

Grace Hayward, born in 1914, lived opposite the pub in the 1920s. Her memories were recorded by the Hastings Local History Group sixty years later. Recalling her childhood when she was about ten years old, she said: 'Our family was strongly anti-alcohol. Our back gate looked out onto the Old King John and on Sundays we weren't allowed to play outside the gate. On Sunday evening all the drinkers used to come and bring their kids and the kids were standing all round the pub and playing and having a lovely time, and we used to watch, and out would come packets of crisps and lemonade and they had lovely dresses on. We used to look on with envy because we never got crisps and lemonade. But we could not understand why our parents used to say "those poor deprived kids, you see they are spending all their money on booze and what will happen now is that the tallyman will be coming for the money for the clothes". I know they were standing outside but they were having a lovely time and they used to make fun of us and we weren't allowed to open the gate and go out. I think [our parents] thought we would be contaminated. Fumes might have leapt across the road.'[5]

In 1962 the licensee, Mrs Minnie Tong, retired after twenty-two years. The magistrate who transferred the licence remarked that this was a sad but historic day as they were 'witnessing a break of fifty years of the Tong family's connection with the Old King John'. On clearing out the pub they found a pistol which was well over 100 years old. It had a horn handle, a barrel that was split and two incorporated blades. They also found a tiny pair of tweezers and a mould for making shot. The ownership and origins of the weapon were unknown.[6]

The Old King John was Alan Crouch's local in the 1960s and 1970s. He described the pub as popular and with very small bars. Because the landlady was asthmatic Alan occasionally took over the bar for her. 'I remember once', he said, 'I poured a drink at 11.30am whilst bottling up and I hadn't finished it at two because it was so busy.'[7] He also played darts for the Old King John in the Fremlin's league in pubs around Hastings, including a memorable match against Denny Gower in the London Trader.

In 1984 this small pub was enlarged when it took over the cottage next door.[8] The pub name is taken from John, King of England from 1199 until his death in 1216. In popular legend he was known as the enemy of Robin Hood and is associated with the signing of the Magna Carta in 1215.

Later he tried to renege on the Magna Carta but this only provoked the barons into declaring war on him. Shakespeare tells the story of his tyranny, treachery and cruelty in *King John*. The artist who designed the pub sign was more optimistic and portrayed him in a more pleasant light.

Pig in Paradise
Palace Court, White Rock

The Pig in Paradise, formerly the Palace Bars, is located on the ground floor of one of Hastings's most prominent buildings. The first building on this site was the Seaside Hotel, built in 1835 which in 1872 became the Seaside and Pier Hotel. It was rebuilt in 1886 as the Palace Court Hotel but like other Victorian hotels in Hastings, the Old Golden Cross or the Havelock, the investment required did not produce an adequate return. Consequently its prices were higher. In 1889 for example, a glass of wine in the Palace cost 6d [2½p] whereas elsewhere in town it was 4½d although the Palace claimed its wine 'was as good as the Bodega' (now the Street).[1] After more investment and alterations in 1894, it reopened 'with electric light in all public rooms' powered by dynamos installed in the caves behind the building.[2]

The wages earned by barmaids came to light in 1891. In that year a barmaid was dismissed for misconduct and applied to the courts for a month's pay of 30s [£1.50] in lieu of notice. The manager, when asked the reason for her dismissal, said she had been kissing the customers. The question is, said the magistrate, 'Did she kiss a customer or did a customer kiss her? Did she kiss or was she kissed? It was established that two male customers had kissed the barmaid which was technically an assault and therefore she could not be accused of misconduct. She received a month's wages in lieu but lost her job anyway.[3]

In the early 1900s the Palace Bars was one of the meeting places used by the Hastings and St Leonards Debating Society, which met to discuss issues of national and local importance. Alf Cobb, local socialist firebrand, was a regular member of the club, which functioned up until the First World War. In 1909 members debated tax the budget and Sunday opening hours for public houses. This was a popular topic with the temperance campaigners who were opposed to Sunday opening.[4] In 1917 the Palace Court Company went into liquidation and the building closed. Struggling financially it was described as 'a thirty year failure' and as 'Hastings's white elephant'.[5]

Nevertheless, Captain Vincent Moss, landlord of the Imperial Queen's Road, took over the bars and restaurant in 1926, after the rest of the building had been transformed into high class apartments. The Palace Bars gained a new lounge designed as 'a bowl of flowers' with giant spikes of gladioli and columns of asters. There were thick pile carpets, a silver service, a Piccadilly chef and wallpaper with a silver tissue pattern over scenes of gondolas. It had a Persian tearoom for 'intimate tête à tête over the tea table'. In the 'swinging twenties' the Palace lounge and the ground floor bars were the place to be seen.[6]

It reopened to acclaim from holiday makers and locals in 1927 and the licensee applied to open up the caves behind the building as a meeting place for the Ancient Order of Druids, who claimed 400 members. Although the caves were fitted out with lighting and ventilation in expectation of being granted permission, the application was refused and the caves were possibly never used.[7]

Pat Dunn remembers the Palace Bars as a smart venue in the 1940s under a head waiter called Lou.[8] Another drinker, Alan Crouch, recalls: 'Sometimes we started off an evening drinking Biddenden cider in the King's Head. Because of its strength you were only allowed two pints. Then we made our way to Hastings pier, which had an extension until 11pm, stopping at the Palace Bars on the way.'[9]

Cyril Pelluet also has good memories of the Palace Bars. 'In the late 1950s', he says, 'it was run by Fuller and Swatland. The head barman was Matthew Hart, a sort of big brother or uncle, always immaculately turned out in a white jacket and slicked back hair. It had a very long bar and the right hand corner was known as Matt's corner. His equally affable sidekick Ted was known as "the stomach in a white coat". The Palace Bars was quite a smart place. At that time National Service was still on and a lot of us servicemen, ex-servicemen, used to meet up there — a happy atmosphere and a lot of camaraderie.'[10]

Twenty-five years later the Palace Bars, now known as the Pig in Paradise, had become an 'alternative' venue describing itself as an 'Ad Hoc Arts and Performance Centre'. In 1984 Roger Carey celebrated his 1,000[th] gig here, with a collection for Ethiopian Famine Relief.

In the mid-1980s, several events were staged from 'quiet music on the Hammond organ and the Bechstein concert grand', to poetry readings, magic, and rhythm and blues. The Pig also hosted the Hastings Free Festival with a 'broad minded selection of culture for the town's alternative masses'. In 1986 the Pig staged two weeks of daily entertainment ranging from radical poetry, blues, country, string quartets, disco synth, craft, free form music, cabaret, comedy and film. It also included psycho sonic music by local band Turn Blue.[11] Numerous other bands performed here including Pass the Cat and Moire Music.

Pissarro's

South Terrace

Pissarro's, formerly known as the Princes, was first licensed in 1864.[1] Among its first customers were visiting cricketers and fans, who came into Hastings for matches on the former Central Cricket Ground, now the Priory Meadow Shopping Centre opposite. The first landlord was Alfred Vidler.

In 1950 the pub sign was featured in Whitbread's series of miniature inn signs.[2] It showed the two nephews of Richard III, who were declared illegitimate by parliament and executed in the Tower of London in 1483. Sometime after 1960, Whitbread repainted the sign to show the princes no longer holding hands.

Mick Nurse was a regular in 1975 and remembers a local fisherman bringing boxes of crabs into the small public bar.[3]

From 1977 to 1981 the licensees were Alan and Marie Garaty, who remember the pub with fondness. 'It was quite a small pub', they said, 'it only had the two bars, public and saloon. Next door, where the restaurant is now, was a furniture depository whose employees were regular customers.'

Marie with customers

They continued, 'We organised wheelbarrow races and a cycle race to Eastbourne, to replace money stolen in a burglary. We had a swear box in the public bar that took a lot of money. All the proceeds went to the children's department of a local hospital. We also ran a successful Princes gun club for clay pigeon shooting on Sundays.'

Marie recalled: 'We never had any really bad incidents, only some minor ones. I used to deal with most of it. But then I was trained by Whitbread to deal with incidents in the bar. The brewery's idea was that a man wouldn't hit a woman whereas he might well attack another man. So they relied on their landladies. But most customers were supportive.'

Sponsored cycle ride to Eastbourne
Marie and Alan are in the centre of the picture

'The building on the other side was a private house. So you see with only two bars we couldn't develop it much further. There wasn't any space for a children's room, something then coming into demand, nor was there any outside space for a beer garden.'[4]

Sometime after 1981 the pub expanded into both the former furniture depository and into the private house next door. In 1992 it was sold and became a freehold premises and hotel. Two years later it was renamed Pissarro's,[5] after Lucien Pissarro (1863–1944) who lived in Hastings briefly in 1918. He painted eight local landscapes, including one of All Saints' Church.

Pissarro's website suggests that it is 'neither pub, wine bar, bistro or restaurant but the best of all of these. A meeting point, a subtle fusion of tastes — visual, audio and gastronomic'. Pissarro's has been voted the south east's premiere jazz, blues and soul venue.[6] But regardless of its new image it still retains the atmosphere of a traditional pub.

On its reopening, the pub rock and jazz scene welcomed its addition to the reduced number of live music venues in the town. At the time the Carlisle was under threat of closure (but was later reprieved), Mr Cherry's had already closed and Blades Club at the Yorkshire Grey was about to close.

Pissarro's was the location of the first Hastings 'Beatles Day' in December 2000. This was designed as a one-off event but was so successful that another date was set for the following April, it being obvious to everyone that a larger venue was needed.

In April 2001, 2002 and 2003 Beatles Day was held at the Marina Pavilion, St Leonards, and Pissarro's became one of the first sponsors. In 2004 Beatles Day moved to Hastings Pier — an excellent venue and home to much of the town's music history. Since 2006 Beatles Day has been held in the White Rock Theatre and this marathon ten-hour event has become one of the most important annual gigs in the Hastings music calendar.[7] 2009 saw the tenth anniversary with 300 local performers. Pissarro's is still a major sponsor.

Local groups who play Pissarro's regularly are Engine, Clutch and Gearbox, Pass the Cat, the Liane Carroll Trio (Ronnie Scott's Award & double BBC Jazz Award winner) and singer Chris Hutchinson (aka the Mellow D Man) whose father Leslie Hutchinson was an outstanding and famous cabaret singer of the inter-war years.

After thirty years Mick Nurse still occasionally visits the pub particularly to listen to local duo Astral Gypsies, a 'folksy group with an edge'.

Another regular is eighty-year-old Dennis Neeves, who plays piano sometimes on Sundays, when the main group takes its interval break. He has been playing piano for several years and also occasionally plays the intervals at Porter's Wine Bar in the High Street and elsewhere.

The current landlord is Sergio Guerreiro, who took over in 2004. He points out that Pissarro's programme is fairly broad but recommends the Dave McMillan band or Desi Valentine for a good evening's music.[8]

Prince Albert
Rock-a-Nore

The Prince Albert, Rock-a-Nore Road, was formerly a fishermen's lodging house, tucked away among the net huts. It was built in 1789.[1] It became the Foresters Arms in 1847 and the Prince Albert in 1852, when it was one of at least fourteen fishing pubs around the Stade. Before the First World War, along with the Nelson, Royal Standard and Dolphin, it was a popular fishermen's pub.[2] The famous Winkle Club, a fishermen's charity for poor children, was founded here in late 1899 and held its first charity supper on New

Year's Eve 1899/1900.[3] The pub is now defunct but its immortality is guaranteed by this fact.

A group of local fishermen who used the pub discussed the idea of raising money for children of poverty-stricken families in the town. In those days there was no welfare state and many working class families, especially throughout the winter, existed in dire poverty and deprivation.

The fishing community decided to organise a self-help charity but were stuck for a name until somebody suggested the Hastings Winkle Club. And so it was. No time was lost in getting the club under way. The history of the club's early days is one of inevitable development. It was decided that every member would have to carry a winkle. The mortal remains of the original occupants of the shells were removed and their places filled with sealing-wax. On being asked to 'winkle up', the luckless person caught without his badge of membership, the winkle, had to pay a fine — a penny in the early days — and the challenger likewise had to report him or pay a fine too. An elaborate system of such penalties developed.[4]

Over the years the club also organised events at the fish market, including festive sports days and banana races, where each competitor had to race with a ten-bushel basket full of bananas on their head. There was also a Winkle Band that marched around Old Town collecting money.

The main event was the children's Christmas party. Ironical then, that the landlord was summonsed and fined £1 in 1920, for allowing children into the room where the Winkle Club was in session, although they used a side entrance.

This type of charity was not unique to Hastings. Mass Observation's, *The Pub and the People* mentions similar charities called Dolly Clubs operating from pubs in the north of England, where every member had to carry a small dolly or pay a fine. Equally another Hastings pub, the Royal Oak, had an Acorn Club, where members were required to carry an acorn at all times.

In the 1930s a second Winkle Club was formed, at the Tivoli Tavern in Silverhill.[5] Both clubs operated on the same principle but with one major difference. The Tivoli Winkle Club had several female members whereas the Hastings club was exclusively male and banned women from its ranks.

Cyril Fletcher wrote a poem poking fun at the men only rule. Here is a verse from it: —

Bessie from an Old Town pub
Had joined the famous Winkle Club
When Winkles Up was cried with zest
She raised hers higher than the rest.
She wore her winkle night and day
She wouldn't put the thing away
Even when swimming in her vest
The winkle glistened on her chest.[6]

With 150 members, the club continued until the Second World War when it closed, except for two concerts organised for evacuee children billeted in the town. In 1948 the Winkle Club held its first dinner for nearly ten years because of wartime food shortages. The Prince Albert closed in 1954 and its licence was transferred to the Duke of Wellington in the High Street The Winkle Club moved to the Jolly Fisherman until 1959. It moved again to the Lord Nelson until 1964, when it finally found a new home at the Fishermen's Institute where it remains to this day.

The Winkle Clubs of Hastings were thereafter remembered by an unusual pictorial link between Hastings and Basingstoke in Hampshire. In 1967 a pub sign was commissioned and designed for a new public house in Basingstoke called the Winkle. This pub is located on Winklebury Way near the Iron Age camp on Winklebury Hill. Its sign shows a winkle shell, the Hastings town arms and a silhouette of Winston Churchill gazing out across the English Channel

The Hastings Arms represents Hastings as the chief Cinque Port The winkle represents the historic Winkle Clubs, while Winston Churchill is included as he was an honorary member of the Winkle Club and Lord Warden of the Cinque Ports.[8]

The Prince Albert is now the Mermaid Café adjacent to Winkle Island, and a monument of a winkle shell.

Prince of Wales
Western Road, St Leonards

The history of the Prince of Wales in Western Road follows a pattern common to many St Leonards pubs. Originally a bakery, it started selling beer in the 1850s and in 1855 was listed in the directory as a simple beer house, when George Sutton was the landlord.[1]

By 1858 it was known as the Prince of Wales.[2] The next landlord was John Snelling, who applied for a full licence which was refused in 1862.[3] He had other businesses in Western Road and was the proprietor of a livery and private stables servicing the residents of the emerging Warrior Square.

Other trades in Western Road at the time included blacksmiths, undertakers, coach builders, washerwomen, saddlers, corn and forage contractors and a bath chair man, all of whom would have used the pub.

Other customers included the men who unloaded the colliers hauled up onto the beach opposite London Road and the carters who delivered the coal locally.[4] As 'bona fide travellers' the men crewing the boats could legally be served out of hours whereas the carters couldn't. This aspect of the law led to much trouble in the local pubs.[5]

A collier delivering coal to St Leonards in 1854

One Sunday morning in 1864 a police constable saw some men standing outside, drinking out of hours. On seeing the constable they went inside. He followed and they exited into the yard at the back. He continued to follow and found them in the kitchen of the house next door with pots of beer. The next door neighbour told the policeman: 'They have only come to look at my cage birds and the beer was delivered from the Old England yesterday!'[6] On other occasions the same policeman was met with 'several expressions of a violent and vulgar character' from some customers.

As the years went by, the Prince of Wales beer house occasionally came up in the local news. In 1878 the *Hastings and St Leonards Chronicle* reported on a secret campaign carried out by a private detective into the town's beer houses. The object was to spy on beer houses that were thought to be selling spirits illegally. The Prince of Wales was caught out when it served rum to the detective. He had been hired by the Hastings Licensed Victuallers' Association, whose members all held full licences. However, when the case went to court it was dropped over a technicality.[7] On another occasion the pot boy had his trousers stolen from the kitchen by an old man called John Love, who was a fern hawker. The police caught Love later in the day in Hastings and the potboy got his trousers back.

After the Second World War the pub was allowed to sell wine as well as beer but was still prohibited from selling spirits. The pub applied for a full licence in 1949, but was refused on the grounds of poor interior decoration.

The brewers replied that: 'Some landlords prefer a bare floor and some customers prefer benches and forms, to plush seats'. But it did apparently need some decoration and new interior fittings, which were near impossible to purchase after the war.[8] At that time it had two small bars.

Pat Dunn recalls that in the 1950s they did bed and breakfast. 'They had a small sign up: 'B&B 7/6d' [37½p] and the landlady played piano'. More than forty years later Pat was barmaid there herself. 'There were characters, of course. One I remember was "Nobby No Toes" who somehow had lost his toes.'[9]

The Prince of Wales is a common pub name but the pub sign in this case refers to Edward the Black Prince (1330–1376). The three plumes of ostrich feathers are from his coat of arms. There were three other pubs with the same name in Hastings but their signs referred to Queen Victoria's eldest son. One in Pelham Street closed after the First World War and another in Bohemia Road closed in 1971. There was also a Prince of Wales Beer House in Old Town around 1865.

Priory
32 Station Road

The Priory, formerly the Royal George, was a pub associated with Hastings railway station and its employees, and with the former Central Cricket Ground, now the Priory Meadow Shopping Centre.

The Royal George was originally an ordinary beer house serving the staff and passengers of the railway station, which opened in 1851. It was granted a full licence in 1864 and the first landlord was George William Thwaites. In his application he claimed his pub was different from the Old Golden Cross (now Laila) on the adjacent corner, which opened in 1857. 'We cater for the middle class excursionists,' he said, implying a hint of snobbery.[1]

The pub seemed to have got off to a good start, selling 400 barrels of malt liquor in its first year. But the idea that it was a middle class house quickly evaporated when it developed a reputation as a 'house visited by tradesmen on tramp', particularly bricklayers, carpenters and plasterers, who travelled between towns looking for work. Whether they lodged in the pub is unknown.

Other customers were day visitors who arrived by train and who could legally be served as 'bona fide travellers' outside normal hours. The pubs were open to them on the production of a rail ticket. In the 1860s Hastings magistrates complained that public houses, particularly near railway stations, were being kept open on Sundays because of excursionists.[2]

The Royal George was also a railwaymen's pub and by the early 1890s it had become the meeting place of the Hastings branch of the Amalgamated Society of Railway Servants. The members campaigned for a 'fair day's pay for a fair day's work' and for a reduction of the long hours worked on the railways at that time.[3]

In 1899 the pub applied for a 6am licence, to be extended to 5am in summer. This was in order to serve the employees of the station and of the goods yard opposite, some of whom worked all night and, as the landlord said, were entitled to an early morning pub as much as the workers in the fish market were. The application was refused.[4]

During the First World War the government was particularly concerned about the amount of alcohol being consumed and in 1915 announced several measures it believed would reduce alcohol consumption. A 'No Treating Order' lay down that people could not buy drinks for each other, especially soldiers. The following year the landlord of the Royal George was cautioned and a customer was fined a massive £5 for supplying a Canadian soldier with two quarts [four pints] of beer.[5]

For the next fifty years or so nothing much is heard about the Royal George but at some point it expanded into the house behind. In 1964 Watney's set up a pub football league in Hastings and customers of the Royal George, the Old England and the Belmont formed the first organising committee. This football tradition continued for many years and was later organised by Roger Povey.

In the late 1980s the pub changed its name to Grace's Wine Bar before becoming the Priory in August 2000. However, its sign shows an early batsman in action, which has an interesting story attached.

Roger Povey ran a Sunday league football team out of Grace's Wine Bar in the late 1990s. When a new landlord decided to change the pub's name to the Bat and Ball because of its location near the old cricket ground, Roger says: 'I obviously couldn't call the team after the new name as it wasn't, I thought, a suitable name for a football team. I had to register the team name and decided to call the team Sporting Priory. It was only then that the new landlord considered that perhaps he should call the pub the Priory for the sake of the team and after the old priory that once owned all the land in the area. I think this is the first time a pub has changed its name to the name of a football team'.[6]

However, the new pub sign had already been painted and showed a cricketer in action over the name Bat and Ball. The name on the sign was changed to the Priory but the figure of the cricketer however, remained.

None of this should be confused with the nearby Cricketers (now the Hastings Terrace Club), another pub which experimented with the name Priory in 1996, although it seems to have been a passing phase.

The Priory closed in 2008.

Queen Adelaide
West Street

The Queen Adelaide came into existence as a beer house in the 1830s, although the building is much older. In 1855 the *Hastings and St Leonards Chronicle* reported a case where the landlord was summonsed for selling rum. The journalist who attended the court described the scene: 'The landlord, Henry Kenward, an old man with a smiling, sleepy countenance, wished to know who had got anything against him. When he recognised the witness he said, "Oh it's you is it, go ahead then". He then said, "I didn't know anything was going on wrong". When the customer bought the rum the landlord was asleep in his chair and his wife said to her loving spouse, "Come on aren't you going to wake up tonight?" Which was answered by a snore.'[1]

A common custom in this beer house was 'tossing for pots'. In 1857 a small group of customers were 'tossing' when a tired fisherman ended up winning four pots of beer in a row. After drinking his four pots he fell asleep with his head between his knees and was robbed. All that was found was his small moneybag, empty in the closet. It was socially acceptable to take a nap. Sleeping in these small beer houses wasn't frowned upon or unusual. Other cases were reported in the Cutter and the Hastings Arms.[2]

In 1863 the landlord, who was also a fish dealer, was charged with serving beer at ten to six on a Sunday morning. He claimed it was his 'custom to open the pub at 4am for coffee'. The constable who reported him said: 'There was no coffee, only eleven men drinking beer'.[3] Despite this the Queen Adelaide was granted a full licence in 1870,[4] followed by permission to open at 5am in 1872 along with other fishing pubs, such as the Anchor and the Queen's Head, who served the fishermen and the workers of the fish market.[5]

Later, in 1872, it was charged with illegal opening again. A drinker who was summonsed said he was drinking coffee 'with three quarters of an inch of froth on it', another that he had gone there to collect his laundry, while the landlord said he was only serving himself!

On a Sunday in 1884, a policeman observed a woman illegally buying brandy in a teacup and carrying it away. In his defence the landlord said he had gone out to get some sand from the beach and the woman had slipped in. 'She needed the brandy because she was ill', he said. The sand was used to cover the floors of the taproom and the public bar instead of the usual sawdust. He was fined for 'serving during the hours of divine service'.[6]

With the onset of the First World War, the Defence of the Realm Act imposed restrictions on the opening hours of all pubs. The Queen Adelaide and other fishing pubs were further restricted by the removal of their early morning licences in 1915.[7] After the end of the war the Queen Adelaide applied to have its 5am licence restored but was refused.

However, it was informed that under the 1872 Licensing Act it could serve 'bona fide travellers' out of normal hours, and the magistrates decided that fishermen returning from fishing trips were just that, and so their crews could be served. But the fishing community was warned that this did not apply to the Hastings ferryman or to employees and others on pleasure boats. The ferryman plied between the beach and boats anchored off shore, ferrying goods delivered by sea. However, this created some discord in the fishing community. Whilst fishermen could legally drink as 'travellers', boys ashore — that is crew members who worked ashore — fish buyers and market traders, could not.

In 1936 a dividing screen between the two bars was removed at the request of the police, so that they could observe the whole of the pub by looking through the window.[8] The police seem to have been unaware of the law: the 1910 Act specifically required fully licensed pubs to have two bars.

In recent times the Queen Adelaide was the only pub in Hastings which opened at 6am, to serve those employed by a depleted fishing fleet. Its licence was the last early morning licence in Hastings. It opened at this time everyday of the week. But, unlike 130 years earlier, this was not enough to keep the pub viable and, sadly, it closed in September 2008.

The Queen Adelaide may have been named after the consort of William IV, as shown on the pub sign or possibly after an eighteenth century revenue cutter built by local shipbuilders Ransom & Ridley. Nevertheless, Queen Adelaide's portrait stood proudly in the corner of the bar. A plaque in St Leonards marks her visit here in 1837.

Railway and the Royal Hotel
St John's Road

The Railway Inn opened in 1854 as a beer house and got a full licence in 1862. Its first landlord, Fredrick Campbell, was supported by two certificates of character including one from 'an influential inhabitant of Maidstone', the location of his previous pub.

This was just as well as the chief constable had heard that the Railway Inn had been 'rebuked by a gentleman of high position in St Leonards', following the wedding of a local brickmaker whose workmates 'behaved in an indecent manner causing a complaint'.[1] The Railway got its licence but Fredrick Campbell was warned that it could be withdrawn at any time. He heeded the warning and no more bad news was heard of the Railway.

In 1876 his wife Mary Campbell, now a widow, took over the new hotel, which had been built on the adjacent corner. At first she called it the Railway Hotel.[2] This was a bad move, as having a Railway Inn and a Railway Hotel within a few yards of each other was obviously not a good idea and it was soon renamed again, this time to become Mrs Campbell's Hotel, 'two minutes from the sea'.

In the late 1870s Hastings was once again visited by the military in the build up to the Anglo-Zulu wars in South Africa. The 'billeting question' was a contentious issue with publicans, who were legally required to provide cheap accommodation for soldiers, at their request. In a court case of 1877, Starr vs. the army, a claim was made for a soldier billeted upon Mrs Campbell's Hotel. She claimed she could not accommodate him and a servant was sent with the man to find him a bed at the soldier's allowance of 4d a night [1½p]. The soldier was found a bed at Mrs Starr's guest house down the road But Mrs Starr thought that 1s [5p] was a more reasonable rate, took the case to court and won.[3]

In 1884 the hotel changed hands and was renamed again as the Royal Hotel,[4] after the nearby Royal Concert Hall (originally the Warrior Square Opera House) and now the site of Royal Terrace flats

The Railway, meanwhile, shot to fame when one of its customers was summoned to a coroner's inquest in 1891. Early one morning, the body of a young girl was found deep in Bo Peep railway tunnel. She was carried to the station and identified as a girl named Polly from Alexander Road, who worked as a domestic servant in Warrior Square

At the inquest, witness's contradicted each other. Suspicious circumstances created a great deal of interest and a large attendance of the general public. The town held its breath while the inquest was adjourned three times.

A doctor stated: 'She died in the night from a large wound on the head. Her handkerchief was saturated in blood but it was dry and tale, about a week old. Had I seen the body in another place I would not have the opinion that she had been struck by a train. There were no marks of a struggle, only blood.'

Station employees suggested that she could easily have walked into the tunnel at night, but couldn't explain why anyone run over by a train would have an injury to such a small area of the body. She was found lying between the rails, but her fingers were stained as though she might have crawled some distance before dying. No train doors were open so she could not have jumped, and all the engines were clean. Her hat was lying beside her.

The inquest was told that she had claimed her employer had ill-treated her. Her employer claimed that she had secretly left his house in Warrior Square at 10.20pm on the night she died, after which time he was drinking in the Railway. The inquest found the evidence wholly unsatisfactory and concluded that she was 'found dead with no evidence to show the cause of death'. Was she killed by her employer and dumped in the tunnel before he went drinking in the Railway? Did someone else kill her, or did she commit suicide? The mystery remains unsolved to this day.[5]

The Royal Hotel suffered a severe blow during the First World War, when the landlady was charged under the 'treating' regulations of the Defence of the Realm Act. The barmaid served a soldier and his girlfriend in the private bar, through a service window that didn't always allow sight of the customers. The police claimed the barmaid had served the soldier with more than one drink, one for himself and

one for his girlfriend. This was 'treating', an illegal act in the First World War, for which they were charged. Although there had been no complaint against the Royal in living memory, the landlady was fined a massive £30 (£10 for each of three offences). According to the historic retail price index, £30 in 1915 would be about £1,600 today.[6]

Then, in 1919, it was the Railway's turn. Food and drink inspectors visited several pubs incognito asking 'for a drop of whisky', which they then examined for quantity, strength and price The Railway was fined £5 for overcharging, after barmaid Elizabeth Shoesmith made the unfortunate comment: 'We have to make big profits because of the rates.'[7]

Pat Dunn, who was born in 1931, recalled: 'I was bought up in St Leonards and the Royal Hotel was one of the pubs used by my family. They drank in the saloon bar from about 1926 and I used to go there as a child. I was allowed to sit in the corner with a lemonade if I kept quiet. I started drinking there myself in about 1947, when I drank ginger wine. At that time it had three bars — a large public bar a small private bar and the more upmarket saloon.

My parents also used the Railway during the war years and after I think it was just one bar and a jug and bottle. My mother told me that when the sirens went off during the air raids they would all go down into the cellar. That's when she started drinking pints so she didn't run out. I remember one local character Bill Elf and his friends drinking at 11am one Sunday morning, a good hour before opening time. When the police came in he joked with them: "We are a committee meeting of the underwater sky diving club", he said and got away with it.'

The Railway was used by the performers from the Regal Theatre (now Ocean House office block), which towers above Warrior Square station on London Road. Stars who performed in the variety shows there included Leslie Hutchinson (Hutch), the famous cabaret singer of the interwar and post-war period. His son Chris Hutchinson sings in Pissarro's today.

In the 1960s the Railway was run by Carl and Judy Burton. In the 1980s Jim and Di Davidson came from the Cambridge to run it They ran it well and Di was a 'no nonsense' landlady.[8]

Cyril Pelluet, remembering the 1960s, remarks: 'As teenage jazz fans, one of the clubs we went to was the Railway Workers Social Club [British Rail Staff Association] opposite the Royal and just a few yards up from the Railway. Every so often, on a Saturday evening, the Dolphin Jazz Band would play there, at which time it was open to the general public and not just to bona fide railwaymen — presumably to boost funds with the bar takings. I'm sure they served 'Grotney's' Red Barrel. Occasionally, there would be guest musicians as well. I'm pretty certain the singer Beryl Bryden played there with the Dolphins on one occasion. I think they also featured other bands from time to time, such as pop/rock bands from the emerging sixties pop and rock revolution.'[9]

Of course jazz fans and others who didn't want to drink 'Grotney's' went across the road to the Royal or the Railway.

From 1931 until 1953 the Royal was tied to Edlin's Brewery, Brighton. Following this it was tied to Tamplin's and then to Charrington's. It is now a free house with all the original bars now one. The Railway still has brown glazed tiles indicating it was once tied to Fremlin's.

Red House

Emmanuel Road

The Red House was built in the mid-1870s as a small hotel, in the new development of the West Hill estate. It has an attractive corner turret — a common feature of local domestic architecture — and is now a private house.

The Red House was first fully licensed in 1876[1] and quickly became renowned for its comfortable, middle class hotel accommodation and facilities. During the late 1880s and 1890s it developed a reputation as a musical house where customers sang and played musical instruments at 'harmonic evenings'. It was advertised as 'three minutes from St Clement's Caves and the lift to George Street, with a lyric club every Tuesday and accommodation for bean feasts'.

By the mid-1880s however, the Red House was beginning to suffer from the effects of the economic depression and trade started to fall off. Like many other pubs it ran a savings club. This one was known as the West Hill Benefit Society and had over 100 members. It paid out a lot of sickness and unemployment benefit in the hard times towards the end of that decade.

The Red House Harmonic Society carried on for a number of years until it finally amalgamated with the Harmonic Society of the King's Head, Old Town, Hastings's oldest pub. The amalgamated society alternated between the two pubs for 'harmonic Saturday evenings' during the final years of the nineteenth century.[2]

One evening in 1894 the society hosted a beef pudding supper and musical programme for its members. Herr Jeckel, a native of Coblenz, sang Monte Carlo, accompanied by the piano. It was reported that 'his broken English added charm to the song'.[3]

By the time of the Edwardian era, the Red House was drawing custom from members of both the Liberal and Conservative parties, who held political meetings here, and from the local bowls club. But by 1903 it seems to have become a radical house, with a Liberal landlord who chaired meetings to discuss, among other things 'the coming of the trams to Hastings'.

At the turn of the last century it was competing with several other pubs within a few hundred yards. These included the Plough and the Manor (which are still extant) and the Little Brown Jug, Whitefriars, Angel and Edinburgh Castle which have all closed.

However, the nearest public house of the same class was the Langham, a mile away.

Just before the First World War the chief constable opposed the renewal of the Red House licence on the grounds of redundancy, when the magistrates queried a fall off in trade. It was pointed out that 'the interior accommodation was extremely good', that it had some 'jug trade' and organised a popular bowls club. A customer with a sense of humour, who appeared as a witness, said the fall off in trade was because, 'the landlord had changed his politics. He got a little controversial.' [Laughter in court.][4]

In 1917 the landlord, James Brown, was called up by the Hastings Military Tribunal, although he 'could not do much walking'. The Tribunal exempted him for one month only, to allow the transfer of the licence to his wife.[5] However, he survived and continued as landlord until 1922.

In 1921 the Red House was offered a handsome compensation of £3,000 if it would close down, but the brewers successfully appealed. Smith & Co., family brewers of Lamberhurst, sold the pub for the same amount to Kemp Town Brewery of Brighton in the same year.

In the Second World War the Red House was lucky. The Emmanuel church across the road was a prominent landmark for German bombers but neither the church nor the pub suffered any damage.

Percy Gardener was the landlord for its last twenty-eight years until 1953, when it was finally declared redundant. He was ill in his final years and had to be brought into court on a stretcher. During 1951 the police visited every pub within a quarter of a mile to establish the custom. All of the pubs had an average of between seven and sixteen customers except the Red House, which had only two.[6]

Roebuck

High Street

The Roebuck, an old coaching house, was situated next to Bourne Passage (now Roebuck Street). Formerly the Starr, it originated from a brewery occupied by Thomas Hovenden from around 1760. It was licensed in about 1800 and on becoming a coaching inn in 1842, changed its name to the Roebuck after a privateer, a ship of the same name.

'The privateer was commissioned as a "man of war" under "letters of marque", to cruise against French, Spanish or "rebellious colonial" ships (i.e. American ships) and to take any goods, wares or merchandise from them.' In other words they had government permission to engage in piracy on the high seas. The crew of the Roebuck was recruited at the George Inn, High Street.[1]

The pub's nineteenth century customers, apart from the stagecoach drivers and their passengers, included the ostlers and stable boys who worked in the stables in Roebuck yard at the rear of the building. In 1854 a carter arrived at the stables to collect a load of dung. It was disagreeable and hot work and the landlord gave him the usual pots of beer and several measures of 'bull'.

'Bull' was a drink concocted by the landlord, by swilling boiling water in gin hogsheads, rum barrels and brandy casks and mixing it together 'for fishermen when they returned from a voyage'. The landlord didn't know the strength of 'bull' but it was literally a killer. The carter died within a few hours of drinking it, but oddly enough at the coroner's inquest which followed, the landlord was only cautioned.[2]

In 1860 the Victoria Tavern, a beer house opposite, was granted a full licence. The Roebuck, then a century old, complained that it would lose custom. With the Mason's Arms described as 'a tramps' lodging house next door' there were now three pubs within a few yards of each other.[3]

In the 1880s it became the headquarters of the St Clement's Bonfire Boys, who organised for bonfire night and held socials and dinners here. Another group, the St Clement's Harmonic and Tradesmen Society, met here weekly 'for social intercourse, vocal and instrumental harmony'.[4]

The pub was a privately owned free house until 1894 when it was sold to A.F. Styles, the Kent brewers, who owned it for four years.

In 1895 the old house was about to be pulled down and new plans were submitted, but for some unknown reason nothing happened.[5]

In 1915 the landlord was called up into the army and sent to war. In 1917 the new licensee fell foul of the Defence of the Realm Act which stipulated that all pubs had to close at 9pm. At 12.30 one night, a policeman saw a light on and three people in the bar. The three people were the potman, his wife and his brother — a soldier on leave from France. The landlord, Frederick Peppin, was charged and fined £10 for 'allowing people in licensed premises during prohibited hours'. The soldier was fined 1s [5p] 'as he might not have known about the law'.

Tenants of other Hastings pubs similarly convicted (the Fountain in St Leonards and the Jenny Lind, for example), lost their licences and were replaced by the brewery. In the case of the Roebuck, the brewers were at first lenient because Peppin's wife was dying of cancer.

Two months after this incident, a priest from a Jesuit college on the Ridge, Ore, was seen buying two bottles of beer before the official opening time. In court, Peppin produced a letter from a doctor stating that an invalid priest at the Jesuit college had been ordered to drink beer twice a day with his meals. This was a common practice although the court didn't accept it, and he was fined again. This time he was fined a massive £50 and the priest £5. For these offences the landlord was described as 'a traitor to the nation' and lost his licence.[6]

The chief constable described the pub as an 'ill conducted premises', and closed it down in 1918 'as a warning and example' to the other licensees of Hastings and St Leonards.[7] Frederick Peppin, who had lost his wife from cancer, his licence and his pub, disappeared from the town and the life of the Roebuck came to a very sad end.

Royal Albion
Marine Parade

The Royal Albion stands on the site of Whitby House, built in 1689 and licensed in 1730. The house was rebuilt in 1831 and reopened in 1832 as the Albion Hotel,[1] a coaching inn on the fashionable Marine Parade. Excellent stabling and lock-up coach houses were available at the rear of the hotel, in George Street.

At that time, the Albion often suffered from bad weather and high tides from across the road. Consequently, in 1836, tempestuous weather and a hurricane blew the windows in. Again in 1855 during a great gale and storm, the sea reached George Street and was so fierce it dislodged the York paving slabs on Marine Parade and threw them against the Albion 'like bits of wood'.[2]

From about 1850 to 1880, the Albion's success fluctuated with the rest of the Old Town, which meant the landlord, James Emary, was always seeking other business opportunities. After the arrival of the railway in 1851, he had an agreement with the railway company allowing his flymen the right to ply for hire at Hastings station to the exclusion of some other horse-drawn cabs. He also tried to undercut them by charging lower fares, in a move that caused a lot of local resentment.[3]

In the 1860s the Albion was offering annual subscriptions for its billiards room, which it promoted as a sort of gentleman's club at the rate of 10s 6d [52½p] a year.[4] In the 1870s he became the local representative for the Glasshouse Colliery of Stoke on Trent and started selling and delivering coal on their behalf.[5] Coal was delivered by colliers to Hastings beach opposite (see illustration on page 156).

In common with some other hotels, the tap room at the rear of the building in George Street, known as the Albion Shades, was granted a separate licence in 1879.[6] During the lean years of this period, the Albion Shades was used by prostitutes, as were the other pubs in George Street (see page 194).

In the 1880s the landlord tried to attract custom from upper class visitors to the town and it was probably at this time that the word Royal was added to the name Albion.

But none of these initiatives were enough to compensate for the poor economy and by 1894 the life of the Royal Albion as a hotel came to an end, following a pattern in the town.[7] The Palace Court was having difficulties and the Havelock Hotel had closed a few years earlier. A section of the back of the Royal Albion was converted into shops and the hotel became apartments. The magistrates, and no doubt the local population, regretted the inevitable change from hotel to public house with three bars. Four years later there were just two bars, the usual saloon and a public bar with swinging doors to attract the excursionists.

The excursionists would also have been attracted to the nearby Empire Theatre of Varieties, a music hall that opened in Pelham Place in 1899, starring Marie Lloyd and Tiller's Eight Fairy Dancers. Marie Lloyd's father was onetime landlord of the Royal Albion, so visiting music hall stars would have been among the customers. The music hall became a cinema in 1913 and is now the De Luxe Leisure Centre.

The Royal Albion and the Shades closed down for a few months in 1910 and the Shades was closed and compensated in 1915 when it was integrated into the main building.[8] Generally the Albion seems to have escaped the wrath of the military authorities during both world wars, unlike several other pubs of similar size.

In 1963 the Royal Albion had to be evacuated, when a leaking gas main caused a series of explosions followed by a blast, sheets of flame and smoke. Thirty-three people were injured and twenty-two properties were damaged on Marine Parade and George Street. The scene was described as 'an experience worse than the war and like a miniature battlefield'.[9]

Alan Crouch recalls the Albion in the 1980s: 'Nearly all the customers were visitors or holiday makers, particularly in the summer', he says. 'There was a very good pianist in the bar who played in the boogie style of Winifred Atwell, which pulled the customers in. The pub was tied to Younger's brewery of Edinburgh and was their most southerly pub. This link with Scotland explains the bagpipes behind the bar and the tartan designs set into the wall panels.'[10]

The name Albion is a poetic name for Great Britain and comes from the Latin word Albus meaning 'white' as in cliffs.

Royal Standard
East Beach Street

The Royal Standard is a fishing pub opposite the Stade. The deeds of this quaint building date from 1707 when a shoemaker lived there. It became a beer house in 1822 and in 1856 John Webb was granted a full licence. The magistrate was facetious: 'You would rather sell spirits with a licence than without I suppose?' 'Yes Sir', he replied.[1]

This pub has always been used by the fishing community and the bar acts as a sort of seadog parliament where fishermen put the world to rights among the maritime and nautical bric-a-brac.

In the 1880s when pubs were feeling the effects of competition from grocers with beer licences, the Royal Standard started selling tea and groceries. It became the distribution agent for all tea sold in Hastings pubs which at one time amounted to 15 hundredweight [762kg] a week.[2] This was helped, no doubt, by the system of allowances for fishing families (see below).

In 1913 this part of Hastings was described as very 'crowded when the fish come in'. The Royal Standard was one of the early morning pubs opening at 5am for boat crews, boys ashore and fish buyers, who sheltered in the pub waiting for fishermen to call out 'sole buyers' or 'cod buyers'.[3] Other customers included boat skippers, mates and the sub coxswain of the lifeboat.

Three boat crews and their boys ashore (a crew member who worked ashore) had allowances in this pub. The allowance enabled them to drink on credit, until the skipper paid the bill on a 'day of settlement'. Fishermen's wives also had allowances, but with the butcher and the baker, who were paid in the same way.[4] The Royal Standard, the Dolphin, the Lord Nelson and the Prince Albert were considered to be the authentic fishermen's pubs according to witnesses at an appeal. Although there were of course several other pubs in the area used by fishermen.

At this appeal in 1900, the fishing pubs lost their early morning licences on the basis that the fishing industry was in decline due to traditional sailing trawlers being out-classed by new steam trawlers. This meant less fishing and less employment for fishermen. An early licence was again refused in 1915, when wartime restrictions on pub opening hours were imposed.[5]

As a fishermen's pub it had a tough reputation, demonstrated by a particular landlady. In 1920 a customer refused to pay up and threw a two gallon [4½ litre] jar of lemonade at the landlord. He was physically thrown out by the landlady, who held him down by the scruff of his neck until he was taken away by the police. He was sentenced to one month's hard labour.

Nowadays the Royal Standard acts as the base for the marble championships on Good Friday and is popular with visitors to the Jack in the Green Festival on May Day. The festival is based on a tradition which started in the 1830s but died out at the start of the twentieth century. Revived in 1983, it is now an annual event that takes place during the May Bank Holiday weekend and has become a tourist attraction.

Jack is a 'green man', who represents the spirit of the forest. He is covered in branches and leaves, wears a crown and a green face. He leads a procession and is escorted by dancers dressed up as trees. These people are called bogies or spirits and live in dark places. There are several different groups, including the Hastings bogies and the gay bogies. Behind Jack there are groups of drummers and people carrying sponges soaked in green paint, which are used to dab the noses of spectators. The festival ends at Hastings Castle, where Jack is slain and the spirit of summer is released.

The Royal Standard is tied to the Shepherd Neame Brewery of Faversham. The brewery produces a beer exclusively for the festival. The 4.1% Jack in the Green Special is described as pale and golden with a clean, fruity taste. It is brewed with Maris Otter pale ale malt, sun-dried golden oats, gently kilned caramalt and pure local honey. Shepherd Neame brews only a dozen or so barrels for the festival, which are sold in the Royal Standard, Hastings Arms, Anchor, Ye Olde Pump House and the Stag.

The Royal Standard and its sister pub, the London Trader, have a history of flooding by high tides. Flood marks are recorded on the front of the bar with dates of when the sea has come through the door. In 1967 a deluge of rain at high tide brought floodwater three feet [91cm] high. Thirty-five stranded customers had to stand on the chairs and tables.[6] More recently, in 2007, there was a flash flood about a foot deep [30cm].[7] With rising sea levels, watch this space.

The Royal Standard usually means the flag of Queen Victoria. The sign of this pub shows the flag of King Harold, used in the Battle of Hastings in 1066.

Smugglers
White Rock

A drawing of the White Rock area in 1844 shows an open space where the Smugglers is today, although it is listed as the Wellington in *Kelly's Directory* for 1845.[1] On 24th June 1850 Anthony Harvey laid a foundation stone on Robertson Street and after the ceremony the party, accompanied by a band and the builder Richard Cramp, went to the Wellington for a celebratory lunch.[2] In 1852 two employees of Rock's Coach Works, two doors away, went swimming at midnight after an evening in the pub. Only one returned The verdict: 'Drowned whilst drunk'.[3]

In 1868 landlady Sarah Barton was summonsed for 'allowing bad characters to assemble in her house'. A police constable looking through a side door saw nine women and seven men. He asked the landlady if she 'knew what class of females she had got there'? 'No' she retorted, 'but I know they are pert and lively'.[4] Ten years later the pub had become more respectable, with a billiards room serviced by a billiard marker and the usual barmaids and potboy.

In 1891 a shoe black (a 'shoey'), who lodged at the Bee Hive in the Old Town, was drinking whisky in the front bar with two others when he collapsed. The head barman, Edmund Clarke, and the under barman carried him along the passage to the pot room where he lay covered in blankets. When they returned at 11.30pm he was dead. An inquest decided that he had died from natural causes, but they couldn't discover his name and he was buried anonymously.[5]

In 1894 the pub was taken over by Mrs Frances Harvey, the widow of a well-known Hastings bookmaker. The police suspected the pub 'might become a resort of bookmakers and betting men' and she was warned.[6] They need not have worried. Four years later she married the proprietor of Café Monaco next door and the Wellington was taken over by Albert Todd, who was to remain for some thirty years.

Before the First World War, Todd was busy challenging the competition on this part of the front line. In 1914 he protested that the Wellington was losing its middle class customers to the bar of the newly opened Grand Restaurant, opposite Hastings Pier (now the White Rock Hotel). He claimed his pub was their equal and could 'serve all social classes with liquor', indicating perhaps a social change in his customer base.

Advertisement 1920

But then came war and restrictions. No one was allowed to 'treat another person or buy alcohol for soldiers and in 1916 when two recuperating Canadian soldiers wanted a drink, someone went into the Wellington and bought them a bottle of whisky, which they drank in the Palace Bars (Pig in Paradise). This person was fined a steep £20.[7]

After the war, Todd opposed the licence for a restaurant at 38 White Rock, as its customers had, up until then, bought alcohol from him. In 1924 he supported changes in pub opening hours for Hastings and was criticised for it by the local churches and the Temperance Association. In 1926 he opposed the reopening of the Palace Bars, before he retired in 1927.

In 1946 the landlord, James Beaven, was summonsed for serving after hours. In court he claimed: 'We were having a session on spiritualism and forgot the time'.[8] In the same year there was an outbreak of smuggling along the south coast. A Hollington man was fined £300 for smuggling whisky from France and admitted supplying the Wellington with nine cases. This incident accurately indicated the pub's future name; however, for these two convictions James Beaven lost his licence.[9]

The next landlord was Arthur Barber, a saxophonist and leader of the Harmony Aces Dance Band, which included his brother Bill, who played drums. The band started playing at the White Rock Pavilion in 1929 and provided entertainment for the troops during the war. In the 1930s they played on a floodlit raft in the sea between the pub and the pier and also at the West St Leonards Holiday Camp. He retired in 1968.[10]

In 1995 an accident occurred when draymen were making a delivery. After opening the delivery flaps in front of the pub, an elderly woman with poor sight fell into the cellar and sustained bad injuries. Courage, the brewer, was fined £3,000 plus costs.

The original sign showed the Duke of Wellington. After the Second World War it was replaced by a sign of a Wellington bomber, whose pilots were stationed at a local training camp.[11] According to one source, this changed again in the 1970s to the Wellesley Arms, the arms of the Wellington family.[12] Another drinker pointed out that it probably changed because of a post war feeling that reminders of the war should be forgotten. The sign changed again in 1995, to the Smugglers.

Stag
All Saints Street, Old Town

The Stag is first mentioned as a pub in 1836[1] but the building, which is of architectural and historic interest, is believed to date back to Tudor times.

The Stag is known as the former residence of Hannah Clarke, a seventeenth century witch. Two cats and two rats mummified in a glass case, are kept in the bar. A notice in the bar explains: —

According to legend the French raids upon the towns of the Cinque Ports during the middle ages led to new methods of defence being devised, although only Hastings had a form of aerial surveillance. At Hastings a witch named Hannah Clark was employed for the purpose. Riding on her broomstick, together with her two cats, she became a familiar sight and gave advance warning of many assaults. Her cats kept the Old Town free of rats. The iniquitous Hearth Tax of 1622 brought these events to a close. The tax was collected by ruthless men who took all they could find, in lieu of cash. At the Stag, then, as now, enduring hard times, the tax collectors took everything including the gruel bubbling on the hearth. They even took Hannah's broomstick from a ledge in the chimney where she used to sleep above the embers. In despair Hannah left Hastings in search of a new broomstick, but never returned. Her cats remained but from that day they caught no more rats. During the Great Plague of 1665 Hastings suffered like the rest of the country and it was commonly believed that cats and dogs were to blame, and so it came about that Hannah Clark's cats were bricked into the fireplace, on the ledge where they used to sleep.

This legend of Hannah continues at the annual Jack in the Green Festival. A giant effigy of Hannah and her broomstick feature in the procession as well as a Morris dancing troope called Hannah's Cat.

Local tradition has it that the building was once a smuggler's haunt and this is heightened by the existence of a secret passage leading from the cellar to some caves at the back of All Saints' Church. The building has a wealth of oak beams, winding passages and staircases, queer little cupboards, doors which lead nowhere and a chimney so wide that one could climb up it. The old building is reached by a double flight of steps from the high pavement. The pub appears to have had a false front built on to it at some time.

Cupboards on each side of the windows reveal what seem to have been ornate woodcarvings. Two finely-carved roses suggest the house dates back at least to early Tudor times. Some think that it may even have been built in the fifteenth century.

The Stag was also home to some unusual pub games. In the 1980s customer Mark Pennington found an historical reference to a game called 'loggetts'. In 1603 the landlord of another alehouse nearby was 'not permitted to allow cards, dices, tables, quoits, loggetts, scailes, bowles or other unlawful games'. Mark decided to revive it.

The game was played out of doors and was a variation of bowls. A wooden figure of a top-hatted manikin was thrown backwards over the shoulder of one of the players, to decide who started and from where. A peg with a wooden ball attached was hammered into the ground at the spot where the manikin fell. The object was to throw oddly-shaped bowls as near as possible to the manikin. A line of string contained within the ball, measured the distance. Unfortunately, this game has disappeared, probably to a nearby antique shop.

The medieval atmosphere of the Stag has also lent itself to the occult. On Halloween night 1982, sixty people attended a four-hour prayer meeting at All Saints' Church, to combat 'the occult forces of evil' in the neighbourhood. Meanwhile, six people in fancy dress, one dressed as a werewolf, held an 'occult convention' at the Stag, which is just 100 yards from the church. The landlord said: 'They weren't going to do anything. It was a joke.'[2] But the prayer meeting may have influenced the fact that by the 1990s the landlord was taking no chances. He became a member of the Parochial Church Council in 1995.[3]

Street
Robertson Street

The Street is one of four licensed premises in a row including Yates's, Hunny Lu Lu's and the Havelock. Its arched doorway was possibly the entrance to the former music hall that was, at one time, situated above what is now Yates. The number on the facade is the original street number listed for the music hall from the time it opened in 1859 with a popular performance of Handel's *Messiah*.

On 6th November 1861 Charles Dickens appeared at the Music Hall and gave readings from *Christmas Carol* and *The Pickwick Papers*. It was reported that he drew a crowd of maximum capacity, with a large number unable to get in. Two lines of waiting horse drawn carriages stretched up Cambridge Road for half a mile.

The Street has been licensed for many years, although not from when it was first opened in 1858. The first licence was granted ten years later in 1868, to Charles West, former landlord of the Anchor, George Street, 'for the store adjacent to the Music Hall'.[1] It was first known as West's Cellars and the licence was granted on condition that the bar 'would be used as a refreshment room, rather than an ordinary inn and not on Sundays'. The first licence was opposed by the Havelock Hotel, which no doubt feared the competition.

In 1872 it became known as the Cambridge Arms and in 1877 as the Cambridge Arms Wine Vaults. The name changed again in the 1880s to West's Stores and Billiards Saloon and again in 1890 to Bodega Wine Merchants. At that time the premises had private accommodation upstairs for a caretaker.[2]

In 1893 an entrance was opened up in Havelock Road, leading down to the cellars, which had been fitted up as a second bar and billiard room.[3] The licensee at the time was Fredrick O'Hara Hoar, who had been an architect in London and a gold miner in Colorado, where he made a lot of money developing a 'machine for washing gold ore'. He then spent a few years in South Africa buying up gold claims, before ending up as the licensee of the Bodega.

O'Hara Hoar and his business partner Mrs Clifford borrowed £1,000 from the brewers and among other things installed a Battle Shoot as a commercial enterprise. They overspent and became bankrupt with debts of £3,385.[4]

The Battle Shoot was most probably a shooting activity using small air rifles, popular at that time in pubs in the Midlands — an ideal activity for the Bodega cellar. The target was probably a bell

1890

target, 'a metal clock shaped device, with a small aperture in the centre, surrounded by rings. The scoring surface was coated with non-drying paint. A bull through the centre scored five points and rang a bell. Shots slightly off target scored 4, 3, 2 or 1, depending on whichever ring they hit. Once a shooter had finished his six shots, his score was totted up and the surfaces were quickly recovered with more paint.'[5]

In later years a local shopkeeper recalled that in the final years of the nineteenth century this saloon was the 'best known rendezvous in Robertson Street. Here would gather in the forenoon the leading business and professional men and some town councillors, over a morning glass of wine or ale'. An advert from that time describes the premises as a 'celebrated house for old whiskies, vintage ports and champagnes'.[6]

For at least sixty years from 1900, the Bodega maintained a reputation for quality, and other establishments in Hastings measured themselves against its high standards. Bodega wines were considered quality products and regarded as the best that Hastings had to offer.

This reputation continued throughout the Second World War. If you got caught in the town centre when the bombers came, what better than to take a glass in the Bodega. During one air raid in 1944 a middle class woman and her sixteen-year-old daughter took shelter in the Bodega, where they were observed by a policeman drinking port and lime. The mother was cautioned for allowing her underage daughter to take alcohol but explained that it could have been her last drink and her daughter's only drink. She was let off with a warning.[7]

Twenty years later the Bodega still maintained its 'cultivated atmosphere'. Peter Skinner, a customer in the early 1960s, remembers the house from that time. 'We went there quite a lot', he says. 'It was a very civilised place. Local solicitors drank there, sherry and things like that'.[8]

It then became Forte's Wine and Spirit Merchants and in 1968 the York Bars, when the second entrance in Havelock Road was reopened. The cellar, underneath the York Bar, was extended in 1970 to become the Crypt and the name changed again to the York and Crypt Bars.[9] The last name change was in 1990 when it became the Street. The Crypt, now Hunny Lu Lu's has its own entrance.

In 1991 the Street became a music venue. Roger Carey organised successful jazz nights for three years until 1994, with star musicians such as John Etheridge, Mornington Lockett and Claire Hamill 'Everybody expressed great enthusiasm for the club', he said and many have been introduced to jazz for the first time.'

Swan

High Street

The title deeds of the property that became the Swan possibly date back 500 years and the earliest known date is 1523.[1] The original complex comprised a hotel with over forty bedrooms, an assembly room and a courtyard with out-buildings covering an acre of ground. Because the Swan was the main stage coach terminus for London and Dover, there were also coach houses, stabling for fifty horses with lofts over, granaries, a harness room and a head ostler's house in Swan Avenue.

LONDON COACHES

FARES REDUCED!

THE REGULATOR & PARAGON,

Four Inside ' Light Post Coaches, from the Swan
and Castle Hotels, Hastings, every Morning at a
Quarter before Nine o'clock, to the White Horse
Cellar, Piccadilly, Bolt-in-Tun, Fleet-street, and Belle
Sauvage, Ludgate-hill.

Fares Inside .   .   . 12s.
Ditto Outside .   .   . 8s.
A considerable Reduction in the Carriage of Parcels.

Advert 1830

Over the centuries, the Swan was the location for all of
Hastings's important social functions and Cinque Ports formalities
and many could be cited. The following is but one example.

In 1854 a celebration was held for Captain Hugh McClure, who
had made a long and distant voyage to the Arctic in search of the
Northwest Passage. Many had searched for the Northwest Passage,
a navigable channel that was believed to connect the North Atlantic
and Pacific oceans. The search was a long chapter of failure, disaster
and tragedy, but also of heroism and endurance.

A previous explorer, Sir John Franklin, disappeared in 1845 and
several expeditions went out to search for him. In the dreadful winter
of 1847 his ships had become icebound in the Arctic and the crew
perished. Franklin is remembered as 'the man who ate his own boots'.

In his ship named Investigator, McClure was the final explorer
to look for Franklin. In doing so he discovered the fabled Northwest
Passage. He was also the first to cross from west to east, partly by
sledge over the sea ice, and gained the distinction of being the first
to navigate from sea to sea.

The celebration menu was:—

1st course: turbot, cod, mock turtle and oxtail soup.

2nd course: turkey, geese, curried fowl, roast and stewed beef, lamb, mutton, ham and tongues.

3rd course: game, pheasant, partridge, wild duck and hare.

4th course: plums, jellies, creams and custards.[2]

Meanwhile the Swan Shades, attached to the hotel in Hill Street with an entrance in Swan Terrace, catered for working class customers. This building on the corner of Hill Street had originally been a brew house. After Hastings's brewery bought the Swan in 1812, the brew house became the Swan Tap and then the Swan Shades in 1818.

In the 1860s the Swan was criticised by the magistrates for letting rooms to prostitutes who congregated in the Shades. The *Oxford English Dictionary* states that the term 'shades' originated in nineteenth century Brighton, as a synonym for wine vaults, but was also a term used elsewhere as 'oyster shades', signifying the availability of prostitutes.[3] The government Select Committee on Public Houses in 1852, also mentioned shades, where they were described as wine rooms trading as freemen of the Vintners' Company and also used by prostitutes.[4]

On the south-east coast, the name 'shades' was commonly used for taprooms located behind major hotels, of which the Swan was a typical example. Other examples in Hastings included the Albion, Saxon, Castle and Queen's Hotel shades. The existence of a shades enabled the proprietor to keep working class customers and prostitution at arms length, but still discreetly supply the sexual needs of gentlemen customers.

In 1865 the chief constable, dealing with a complaint about the Swan and Castle Shades, remarked: 'It is almost impossible [for landlords] to get a living without resorting to something beyond the ordinary trade'.[5]

In 1879 the Swan was demolished and a smaller, more modern pub built. But the Shades, a separate building, remained until it was reconstructed in 1889.[6]

The year before, a customer in the Swan was fined for threatening a prostitute with a cast iron spittoon[7] and in the same year, 1888, an auction was held to sell off the premises with a reserve price of £7,000. The landlord of the Norman Hotel, St Leonards, bid £5,000, but the highest bid at £6,300 meant it remained unsold.[8]

In 1930 the Swan's licence was opposed by the chief constable on the grounds of redundancy. There were twelve other pubs within 200 yards [183m] and the Swan closed. But on appeal it was reprieved and the licence of the Mitre, a pub on the opposite side of the High Street, was transferred to the Swan, which reopened in 1932 and the Mitre closed down instead.[9] The Mitre, however, regained its licence many years later as the Mitre Restaurant and more recently as Porter's Wine Bar.

In May 1943 the Swan was bombed by a low-flying enemy aircraft and completely destroyed. Eleven customers lost their lives and many were injured.[10] In July, the brewery applied to erect wooden shacks as a temporary home for the Swan, but was refused. Hastings Borough Council protested that to allow wooden shacks would affect postwar town planning.[11] Consequently the Swan was never rebuilt. Its licence was held 'in suspense' until 1946, when it was transferred to a new pub in Hollington called the Wishing Tree.[12] Today a small memorial garden reminds us of this Second World War devastation.

**On this site stood
THE SWAN INN
& 1,2 & 3 SWAN TERRACE
destroyed by enemy action
at about mid-day on Sunday
23 May 1943 with considerable loss of life.**

Tubman and the Dripping Well
Cambridge Road

The Tubman, formerly the Carpenter's Arms, is listed in the directory for 1845[1] and was a beer house for some years before that date. In 1884 it was renamed the Cambridge Hotel.[2] A lot of its history is centred on the upstairs club room, which must be one of the most widely used pub rooms in Hastings. For many years it was the meeting place of printers' and compositors' trade union branches, known as chapels.[3] The printers themselves worked next door in the *Observer* building and at Parsons print works on Claremont.

In the nineteenth century, printers also used the room for smoking concerts. A typical printer's 'smoker' had singers and soloists playing the cornet, mandolin and violin and 'comic recitations', among other acts.

In 1900 it was the room where forty-three local army volunteers received an honorary breakfast, accompanied by speeches from the mayor, before leaving for South Africa and the Boer War.[4] From 1937 the same room was home to the semi-finals and finals of the Annual *Observer* Darts Tournaments, although the Cambridge dart teams themselves were unlucky.[5]

From 1907 until 1934 the landlord, James Bargent, was a well-known Hastings personality. Before the First World War he was the secretary of the London Cab Company. He was a member of the Buffaloes and received every Buffalo honour, including Provincial Grand Primo for Sussex. He ran the refreshment bars at the Central Cricket Ground and at the bowls tournaments at White Rock.[6]

During the Second World War, the clubroom was used to promote campaigns in support of the war effort. In his book *Hastings at War,* Nathan Goodwin says that 1940 was the year that 'Alderman Blackman launched the Hastings Spitfire fund in an attempt to raise £5,000 for a new Hastings Spitfire'. Donations came from all over town including its many pubs. The Cambridge darts team were contributors to the fund. All scores under ten required a halfpenny in the Spitfire tin. Hastings eventually got its Spitfire, known as the 'Hastings', which went to war with a Polish crew about a year later.[7]

Jim and Di Davidson took over in 1961 and for the next twenty years the Cambridge was Hastings's most popular pub. Jim remembers: 'At one time the brewery lorries from Maidstone carried enough beer for four Hastings pubs. At the height of our popularity we had a lorry load of beer to ourselves. Many different people used the pub. All of the Hastings trade union branches met in the upstairs room. These included ASLEF (the train drivers' union), railwaymen, taxi drivers and others. The printers' chapels had always met there.' Hastings Trades Council met there from at least the 1950s to the 1970s.

Jim continued, 'Numerous clubs and societies also met upstairs, including the Cage Birds Society and the Hastings Hill Walkers. In the 1960s when traditional Latin mass in the Catholic Church was banned by Rome, the local congregation hired the big room and held mass there. At first we didn't know what they were doing, but they met there for about two years and had a drink afterwards.

Ed Burra, painter and printmaker, and John Banting, surrealist

The Fantastic BEER ENGINE

57 CAMBRIDGE ROAD • 420074

Every Wednesday Night

Forfeit, Prize & Quiz Nite!

Try a totally fun night out - including the 1 minute Bar Dash

Saturday 1st October 1994 at 8pm

The British Armwrestling Association

Presents

OVER THE TOP

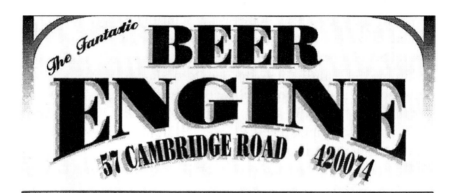

PRIZES & TROPHIES

Mystery Beer Competition!
WIN A MOUNTAIN BIKE

THE ONLY PUB WITH THE

88p-a-pint Recession Session Bitter

If you're looking for something fun & different
Try The Beer Engine!
ONE NIGHT COULD CHANGE YOUR IDEA OF A GOOD NIGHT OUT!

painter, both with work in the Tate, drank there regularly, as did George Melly.[8] Another customer in the 1970s was *Observer* editor, Gary Chapman. The Cambridge was one of his favourite pubs. We were having problems with the high rent charged by the brewery at the time and Gary wrote some criticism about the brewers in the paper. The brewers didn't want negative publicity and "encouraged" us to move, which we did in 1982.'

In the 1960s Peter Skinner was a reporter on the *Observer*. 'One of the regulars', he reminisces, 'was a guy called Frank Rhoden, who ran the Hastings International Chess Congress — one of the biggest in the world. Because of Frank, all the Soviet Grand Masters and people who were legends in the chess world came into the Cambridge during the congress. They dressed up as English parsons in grey flannel trousers, tweed jackets and pipes. They did this because they had a notion of what the middle classes in England were like and they aped it. All these Grand Masters sitting there, looking like country parsons. They wandered down because Frank was the organiser, they came to an English pub and they would play chess with the customers. I played with a number of them.

Probably because of Frank, there was a thriving chess community. I played chess at lunchtimes with printers or other journalists. Jim kept the boards. He was a very easy going and likeable guy. The other thing, it was only 250 yards from the Hastings Chess Club, the only club in Britain which had its own building and which opened from 1pm to 11pm, every day of the week.

The players would walk down to the Cambridge. Hastings has a great chess tradition. I played with Smyslov and a Dutch player, whose name I can't remember. All the great players of the sixties would come in and play. Some of them would play everybody in the pub at the same time, without even thinking about it. But they loved the notion of the pub — an English pub.

It was an eclectic mix of printers, journalists, artists, chess players and darts players. It really was a socially mixed pub. There was no notion of class. Everybody went into the public bar.'[9]

In the early 1980s the *Observer* moved and in 1982 longstanding landlord Jim and his wife Di moved to the Railway in St Leonards. The incoming landlord changed the name to Tavern in the Town and created a nostalgic Victorian atmosphere, supposedly reminiscent of the seaside at the turn of the previous century. The downstairs bars became one and various artefacts including a bathing machine; sign boards and a collage of Victorian seaside postcards were installed.[10] By the mid-1990s the name changed again to the Beer Engine and it is currently a teenage, gothic pub called the Tubman.

Meanwhile, the Dripping Well next door started life about 1850 as a beer house run by Elizabeth Collins, who advertised herself as a 'Baker, Grocer and Beer Retailer'. About twenty years later it was licensed to her son, Joseph Montegue Collins, and acquired the name the Dripping Well.

From 1894 until 1937 the premises were run by Dennis Coppard and were shared with Charles Lane, a wholesale confectioner. Dennis Coppard was one of the longest serving landlords in the town with over forty-three years' service.

Although it was policy to close one pub where two were adjacent, both pubs have escaped this fate. Both are situated on the slope of Cambridge Road and the Dripping Well is built on two levels with one bar overlooking the other. Its name comes from the Dripping Well in Hastings Country Park. The Tubman is named after the runners who carried brandy for smugglers in days of 'yore', so fittingly portrayed on the pub sign.

Warrior's Gate
London Road, St Leonards

One of St Leonards earliest pubs, designed by architect Walter Inskip, the Warrior's Gate opened in 1833[1] when it was occupied by George Hyland. The original building included hotel accommodation and was much larger than the recent pub.

In 1839 the Adelaide Lodge of the Oddfellows was established here, which had 450 members and average annual receipts of £700. In the Lodge Room, each member paid a joining fee of between 5s and 20s [25p–£1] according to age and drew sickness benefit of 12s [60p] a week up to a year, with a free local doctor. The lodge also paid death benefits of £12 and £6 on the death of a wife. It was described as 'one of the most secure investments among the Friendly Societies in the country'.

In a typical initiation ceremony, a new member was blindfolded and taken to the lodge room. His proposer and seconder knocked three times and gave a password to a doorkeeper. A member then shook his hand and asked if he had joined of his own free will. A declaration of principles was read aloud, a litany was chanted and a long clay pipe, a symbol of purity, friendship and peace, was handed to him. With his right hand he pressed the clay pipe to his heart and snapped it with both hands. An oath of secrecy was read out which he repeated. The blindfold was then removed to reveal the chairman in regalia standing on a dais before an altar. All present formed a chain and danced around him singing Auld Lang Syne. This was followed by a welcome speech and drinks all round.

Every Whitsun hundreds of members celebrated with a grand parade. This started at the pub and complete with banners and bands marched to White Rock, where they joined other branches from pubs such as the Anchor, the Crown and the Swan. The day ended with eating and dancing, usually to the music of the St Leonards Quadrille Band, which included Thomas Brett playing guitar and Tom Reed, a 'hard handed violinist and untiring fiddler'.[2] A typical 'soiree' held in 1860 was attended by 120 Oddfellows who had an 'excellent tea' at 4pm followed by dancing 'with other amusements until the following morning'.[3]

In 1917 the building was reduced in size and partly converted into shops and flats. The pub was sited at the junction of Norman Road and London Road. In 1943 the pub was bombed and burst into flames, trapping and killing a number of people. The landlord, his wife and a customer were rescued from the basement.[4] The pub was totally destroyed by the bombing and the brewers applied to erect wooden huts as a temporary measure. They were opposed by the council on the basis that this might hold up postwar town planning. 'If we allow this', a spokesman said, 'we would soon have a town of wooden shacks'.[5] The pub was rebuilt in 1950 on the corner of Shepherd Street, and the post office now stands on the original site.

In the 1970s, darts champion Denny Gower became landlord. He captained the Warrior's Gate darts team into the finals of the Vernon's Treble Top in 1976, and in the following year he achieved two world records — one for playing three games of 301 in the amazing time of 2 minutes 9 seconds. This required each game to be played in forty seconds — the average time most players take to decide what to aim for! The second record was for an 'arm's length round-the-board-on-doubles' feat, which he did in 9.2 seconds. Gower was also Sussex champion from 1968 and overall won 200 silver cups.[6] Pat Dunn recalls that he also played bass guitar with a band. She heard him play in the Angling Club in the Old Town at about this time. Apparently he was a much better darts player than a musician.[7]

At the time the landlord considered changing the pub's name to the Darts Inn, but this never materialised.[8] The pub's first name was Warhouse Gate, after a lime kiln that originally stood on the site. It kept this name for seven years until 1840, when it was changed to Warrior's Gate, the name of a planned Regency housing estate designed by architect Lewis Vulliamy in 1843, on the site of what is now Warrior Square. However, Vulliamy's plan never came to fruition.[9]

In the 1890s it was known as the Warrior's Gate and London Distillery. Its last two pub signs referred to the Norman invasion, as portrayed on a section of the Bayeux Tapestry. In 1950 the sign was included in Whitbread's collection of miniature inn signs.[10]

The pub closed in 2006.

Wheatsheaf and the Bricklayers Arms
Bohemia Road

Bohemia's early history is peppered with the surname of Jinks and many members of the Jinks (extended) family once resided in the district. In the second half of the nineteenth century, at least twenty-five people with this surname, in six family branches, lived along Bohemia Road. Their adult occupations ranged from the building trades, shop keeping (one was a greengrocer), taking in laundry and running pubs.[1]

Bohemia's first pub, the Wheatsheaf, was built by John Jinks, a bricklayer who had previously been a squatter on the America Ground, where he had a ready-made clothes shop. This was approximately where 40 Robertson Street is today (Hoagies Reloaded Café).

When the 'Americans' (see page 76) were given notice to quit in 1835, John Jinks moved to Spittleman's Down, later called Bohemia Place and now a part of Bohemia Road. He built the sandstone wall on the eastern side of Bohemia Road, probably the walled garden, houses in White Rock and Prospect Place and ornamental brickwork in Warrior Square. He was also the first landlord of the Wheatsheaf.[2]

From 1848 to 1911 the Wheatsheaf was run by the Pratt family. In 1856 when the pub was advertised for sale, its stables (now the Pizza Hut takeaway) and skittle alley were especially mentioned.

During the time of the Pratt family, the Wheatsheaf was popular with skilled artisans and respectable tradesmen, who regarded themselves as superior to the unskilled labouring classes. These men, dubbed the 'Aristocracy of Labour', usually wore bowler hats and ties. In the 1870s they set up a number of branches of the Conservative Working Men's Association in Hastings. The Bohemia and Silverhill branch met at the Wheatsheaf and had at least 100 members. Their secretary, George Upton, was also one time landlord of the Prince of Wales.[3]

From 1913 until 1922 the pub was known as Ye Olde Wheatsheaf. In the latter year it was sold by the brewery for £4,000 and reverted back to its original name. In 1917 the landlord was fined a steep £5 for serving a soldier with a bottle of beer[4] and in 1919 he was fined again, this time for overcharging.[5]

A short distance from the Wheatsheaf, a beer house known as the Bricklayer's Arms was located at 21 Bohemia Place from at least 1853 (when it was licensed to a Miss Young) to 1868. In 1865 it was licensed to another member of the Jinks family, Fanny, probably John's niece, a young widow aged thirty-two. She fell foul of the law when she was summonsed for 'failing to admit the police' at 12.15am. When the police eventually got into the house 'they found two men drinking beer in an upstairs room'. The summons was dismissed after a caution with the comment: 'We want to teach beer house keepers that the police must be admitted immediately'.[6]

However, she was summonsed again in 1866 for 'keeping bad time'. Her brother appeared in court on her behalf. 'P.C. Marchant stated that about half-past 11 on Sunday night he was at Bohemia and heard a noise at defendant's house. He went there and on looking in one of the windows, saw several men sitting in the room smoking. He saw one of the men take up a quart pot and drink from it. The door was unlocked and he went into the house. He saw defendant's brother who said their clock was fast enough and that no beer had been drawn after 11 o'clock.' Fanny Jinks was fined £1 with costs.[7]

James Standen is listed as the next licensee in 1867/8 but 21 Bohemia Place is not listed as a beer house after that date. It was most likely a free house as there is no reference to it being tied to a local brewery.

It was probably the case that after two offences the Excise refused to renew Fanny's licence or that she couldn't cope with further scrutiny by the police. Equally, James Standen probably didn't wish to be associated with the name of the Bricklayer's Arms. In any case after 1868 it reverted to an ordinary residential house which later became number 132 Bohemia Road after the road was renumbered.

The 1871 census lists John Jinks (bricklayer) and family now living at 31 Bohemia Place and Fanny Jinks (widow) and family living at 26a Jinks Passage, possibly a twitten off Cornfield Terrace. She was then working as a laundress.

Some time between 1868 and 1871, James Standen became the licensee of another beer house at 29 Bohemia Place. This beer house later became known as the Barleycorn and later still as the Hearts of Oak.

The Pelluet family moved into number 132 in the 1930s and Cyril Pelluet was born there in 1940. He says: 'As a child I always believed the house to be haunted and my father insisted it had been a pub sometime in the past and that there might be a connection between the pub and a ghost.'[8]

Although 132 Bohemia Road is the site of the Bricklayer's Arms, the original house seems to have been rebuilt. The more modern pair of semi-detached houses that stand today do not resemble the small mid-nineteenth century terraced cottages that flank them either side. The Wheatsheaf, now 174 years old, continues to trade. The Jinks surname however, is conspicuously absent from today's Bohemia.

Wishing Tree and the Hollington Oak
Wishing Tree Road, Hollington

In 1943 the Swan Hotel in the High Street, possibly the town's most prestigious pub, was completely destroyed by bombs (see page 195). The Swan licence was held 'in suspense' for three years until 1946 when the Phoenix brewery transferred the licence to Norton farmhouse in Hollington, which thereafter became known as the Wishing Tree public house.[1]

The first pub sign showed a teenage girl on the verge of womanhood, standing under a tree bathed in moonlight, dreaming of marriage. This sign was included in the Whitbread's miniature inn signs collection.[2] The current sign depicts two young females dreaming in an orchard. The tree in question once stood in Wishing Tree Road and there are two theories as to its origin. One relates to a children's game, the other to smuggling.

The former theory came from information at Hastings Museum which claimed that the name Wishing Tree was possibly based on nothing more than a children's game from the 1850s and does not refer to any particular tree.[3] However, in the *History of the Church in the Wood, Hollington,* F.W. Bullock complains that: 'We should guard against the ever present danger of the loss of local names and the substitution of new ones. A notable example is the Wishing Tree, a foolish modern name for a tree implying a story which is non existent.' The old name for the tree, he claims, was Scrag Oak or according to local legend, Smuggler's Oak, from times past when it was a rendezvous for the tubmen.[4] The tree had seats around it, where locals would sit and talk and pass the time of day.[5] Whatever the origin of the name of the tree, it was removed from a small green in the centre of Wishing Tree Road in the early days of the Second World War, when the road was improved.

To confuse the issue further some think the tree in question was the original Hollington Oak, now the name of another pub further down the road. The Hollington Oak opened in 1950 when the licence of the Royal Oak, Castle Street, was transferred to the Southlands Court Country Club.[6] Originally Stone House Farm, it was built in 1740. Thus both pubs in Wishing Tree Road are possibly named after the same local landmark, an oak tree which had been a landmark for generations. The only other pub listed in the area was the long gone Hollington Corner, built in 1833 and noted for the ale brewed by the landlord.[7]

In 1948, a sapling oak was planted to replace the old one. Fifty children joined hands and danced around it singing: *To English Folk the mighty oak is England's noblest tree.*[8] This tree is probably the splendid specimen now on the corner of Redgeland Rise and Wishing Tree Road.

The Wishing Tree public house became well known for its successful social club that existed from 1949 to 1975.[9] In its peak years it organised sports days, carnivals, torch lit processions and bonfire parades on fifth of November. It took over this role from the Bohemia Bonfire Boys, which eighty years earlier met at the North Star. Bonfire night is very much part of the Sussex tradition and for many years the Wishing Tree club had a thirteen-foot 'Guy' inherited from Bohemia.

On fifth of November the procession and the guy would leave the Wishing Tree recreation ground for a torch lit procession into town and along the seafront, accompanied by 300 young people as torch bearers. Its return to Hollington was followed by the burning of the guy on a huge bonfire, thirty feet [9m] high, with fireworks and a barbecue.

The Wishing Tree is another Hastings haunted pub which has been investigated by the BBC. But the ghost this time is different; it smiles, apparently. Several landlords and their families have claimed to have had supernatural experiences. One landlord had an Alsatian dog that went mad when they moved in and had to be put to sleep. Children have been known to laugh at the 'ghost with a funny face'.[10]

A price survey in 1975 found that the Wishing Tree was the cheapest pub in Hastings, but not because it is haunted. The Hollington Oak wasn't included in the survey. More recently, in 1992 the landlady held the world record for picking winkles with a pin. She picked fifty winkles in one minute forty-seven seconds, a record improved on in 1993 by four seconds.[11] The customers then enjoyed them with their beer.

Wishing Tree

209

Ye Olde Pumphouse
George Street

Ye Olde Pumphouse in George Street, at first glance, appears to be one of the oldest pubs in Hastings. However, it is a mere fifty-three years old, having opened in 1956. Before the Second World War it was three separate dwellings centred on a well-known boot and shoe shop owned by two brothers, Sidney and William Carey.

As with many Old Town premises after the war, this complex of buildings lay empty and derelict until sold to a brewery. Fire broke out in 1953 destroying practically the whole of the building, which over the next three years was reconstructed by a Canadian builder called Anthony Newman. Some old timbers from badly war damaged houses in All Saints' Street were incorporated into the front of the building. A written statement by a researcher some years ago notes that the original building was extensively rebuilt 'but this did not quite extend to a new building'. However, details were not given.[1]

Turning modern buildings into 'olde' ones was not so unusual at the time. After the war, damaged buildings were bought up cheaply tudorised' in the style of Mock Tudor and sold at a good profit.[2] Another example of this is the old cottage next door to the Cinque Ports Arms, in All Saints Street.

Regardless of its origins, Ye Olde Pumphouse has maintained its value as a building and in 1982 it was included in 'a million pound deal' by Whitbread, when it purchased a number of pubs in the south-east. Soon after it became a Grade II listed building.

Cyril Pelluet frequented the Pumphouse as a teenager. 'In the 1950s,' he says, 'it was run by Jimmy King and his partner Albert There was only the downstairs bar at that time which was decorated with sailor's hatbands. We liked it because it was frequented by the Teds' or teddy boys and was a local centre of fashion with drape jackets, drain-pipe trousers and DA [duck's arse] hairstyles. This was about 1957/8. Later John Kilroy took over as landlord. An Irishman John had a magnificent handlebar moustache and with his wife Noreen, transformed the upstairs bar into the place to be seen on a Saturday night and it's where we met up with our girlfriends later in the evening. John Kilroy was the epitome of a gentleman and we all had the utmost respect for him. Another landlord, Arthur Wilkinson Bell, introduced curry evenings in the early 1960s, which was quite revolutionary at the time.'[3]

Michael Rose recalls: 'Prior to 1957 when I was on leave from the navy, I used to drink in the Horse and Groom at lunchtime and in the Pumphouse in the evenings before moving on to the pier, which had an extension licence. In these two pubs I would meet up with mates on leave. The Pumphouse had a lot of naval customers then and a collection of naval memorabilia, hats and so on.'[4]

Peter Skinner drank there in the late 1960s, by which time it seems the image had changed. 'The Pumphouse', he believed, 'was more middle class, more conventional, [and served] salesmen and people on the make. The Pumphouse was the pub to meet women. I met my first long term girlfriend there when she was a student from Norway. I spilled some lager over her because I was drunk and that led to one thing and another. We lived together for ten years.

I never saw the Pumphouse as a very old pub, even though it had mock beams and so on. The Anchor seemed much older with its warren of little rooms. The Pumphouse was a harbinger of things to come, a little artificial, a little more knowing and commercial than the other pubs in that area. It was a nice pub, always a little different, not rough, and it was more friendly. Women found it more friendly.'[5]

The pub's name is derived from the site of a freshwater pump that provided this part of Hastings with some good quality water, filtered by the local sandstone. The pump, which never ran dry, is now attached to the front of the half-timbered building and is thought to be 400 years old. Thomas Daniels landlord of the Anchor opposite from 1805, owned the pump in the early nineteenth century. Up until the Second World War, a tax of one penny was paid on the pump every year.[6]

In the past, the pump was a valuable property, producing a substantial income from water sales for the owners. Most other pubs in the Old Town used its pure water and would use no other for the breaking down of spirits. Before the First World War, spirits were supplied to pubs at a high strength and publicans were required to break them down with water. The legal maximum dilution of spirits was twenty-five degrees under proof for whisky, brandy and rum and thirty-five degrees under proof for gin. So as a supplier of pure water, this site has had a relationship with the pubs of the Old Town for more years than it has been a pub itself.

York Hotel
Wellington Place

York Buildings, now a shopping centre, was originally a cluster of private lodging houses. These buildings once looked out over the Priory Bridge and the shanties of America Ground before the construction of Robertson Street from 1850. In 1852 Susannah Osborne was granted a licence for a York Tavern[1] and in 1853 Thomas Coussens appeared to have been granted a licence for a second York Tavern opposite.[2] Not surprisingly, the first York Tavern changed its name to the Freemasons in 1854.

The Albert Memorial, erected in 1862 in front of the York, quickly became the most important landmark of Hastings town centre. By 1866 James Hayter was the licensee and the buildings had become commonly known as Hayter's York Tavern.

The York Tavern was the pub of the boxing community.[3] One of its more famous customers was Tom Sayers (1826–1865), the Brighton-born, nineteenth century champion bare-knuckle fighter, who stayed at the York when in Hastings. In 1857 Sayers became heavyweight champion of England (unofficial, since boxing was then illegal) and was the last holder of the title before the introduction of the Queensberry rules in 1867.

In the 1870s the police became concerned about the numerous fish hawkers causing obstruction outside. Several hawkers were summonsed more than once for allowing the public to gather around their whelk carts at closing time. When a constable asked one to move on he was 'answered in three or four warm sentences, pungent with bad language'.[4]

A fraudulent business scheme referred to as 'the Liberal Association and York Hotel case' in 1878 provoked a local outburst. Controversially, the York was auctioned off on the cheap, to purchasers who knew that Hastings Corporation would have to purchase the property to carry out road improvements. The owners made a large profit at the ratepayers expense. Hayter, a Liberal councillor, probably tipped them off and in 1879 a new York Hotel was erected.[5]

In the 1890s it became known as the York Hotel and London Distillery. The ground floor bars were designed on the lines of a gin palace with fast service from the beer engines and decorated with ornate mirrors and etched glass. In short, a Victorian Wetherspoon's with cheap and plentiful supplies. On the other hand, the lavishly furnished upstairs lounge was described as looking like a high-class club. 'A thick Turkey carpet covers the floor and on the walls a rich Japanese paper has been used, surmounted by a hand painted tulip garden frieze....' The stained glass windows were curtained in gold silk, the bar was walnut and the whole lounge was approached by 'a flight of marble steps'.[6]

The York applied several times to have its off-licence at the rear of the building in York Gardens changed. As an off-licence it could only sell liquors and wines in bottles. The landlord claimed that customers often wanted to taste the wine before buying and had to go round to the bar. The applications were always refused.[7]

The upstairs lounge of the York Hotel and London Distillery

During the First World War, the licensee was charged with allowing soldiers to get drunk. The police claimed that he was not a fit and proper person to run a public house and opposed his licence. They also claimed the York was used 'by low class women and persons of bad character' and 'by some of the worst persons in the town who were in and out all day long'.[8]

A renewed licence was at first refused but then allowed, although the magistrates noted a complaint by the local commanding officer that large numbers of the Royal Field Artillery were being arrested for drunkenness in the town centre. The evening street scene outside the York was described as a drunken 'khaki crowd'. Soon after, a new manager was appointed.[9]

The York was also popular with the military in the Second World War. Retired Police Inspector the late Charles Banks recalled that 'Hastings police were once called to the York Hotel. There, a G.I. got into a quarrel with two English soldiers and the American had suddenly drawn an automatic pistol from his tunic and fired two rounds into the pub ceiling. The two English privates quickly disarmed the G.I. ... and he was detained in a police cell. The G.I. was charged with "carrying a concealed weapon"; recklessly firing two rounds into the York Bar and disorderly conduct. After a full hearing he was sentenced to twelve months imprisonment.'[10]

The upstairs lounge of the York was still popular in the 1950s and early 1960s, especially with courting couples.[11]

In 1964 the lease on the York Tavern came to an end and the licence was transferred to Falaise Hall in White Rock Gardens. The two upper floors were removed and the lower floors became Hastings Information Centre. It is now Costa Coffee.[12]

The Albert Memorial clock tower synonymous with the York Hotel as the centre of Hastings since 1862, was demolished after a fire in 1973.

Reference Notes

The following abbreviations have been used in the references:

HBC   Hastings Borough Council
History Group   Hastings Local History Group
History Workshop   Hastings Modern History Workshop
HSLC   *Hastings and St Leonards Chronicle*
HSLG   *Hastings and St Leonards Gazette*
HSLN   *Hastings and St Leonards News*
HSLO   *Hastings and St Leonards Observer*
HRL   Hastings Reference Library
PHS   Pub History Society
ROL   Register of Licensees

Admiral Benbow
1 Brett v1 p86
2 HSLO 23/3/1905
3 Hastings Directory 1884
4 HSLO 13/8/1898
5 HSLO 4/6/1993
6 Trefor Holloway interview 2009
7 thecopperfamily.com

Anchor Inn, East Ascent
1 Brett v1 p97
2 HSLC 31/8/1881
3 HSLO 10/2/1906

Anchor Inn, George Street
1 Manwaring-Baines 1986 p361
2 Brett v3 p170
3 HSLN 16/6/1848
4 Brett v6 p214
5 HSLC 28/6/1871
6 HSLC 25/10/1876
7 Cyril Pelluet interview 2008
8 Michael Rose interview 2009
9 Pat Dunn interview 2009

Angel and the Plough
1 Manwaring-Baines 1986 p361
2 Census Return 1841
3 HSLC 15/2/1860
4 HSLC 30/8/1871
5 Matthews 2003 p63
6 HSLO 12/2/1921
7 HSLO 26/7/1977

Barrattinis's Sports Bar
1 HSLO 7/6/1975
2 HSLO 2/12/1975
3 HSLO 9/1/1981
4 HSLO 21/1/1984
5 HSLO 21/4/1988
6 HRL pub files
7 HSLO 5/7/1990

Bo Peep
1 Brett HB v1 p98,
2 Manwaring-Baines 1986 p361.
3 Prothero v3 p261, v4 p349
4 Brett v3 p265
5 Brett v3 p294
6 Brett v6 p173
7 HSLC 22/8/1877

Bulverhythe
1 Sussex Directory 1855
2 HSLO 31/3/1900
3 HSLO 7/5/1910
4 Pat Dunn interview 2009

Carlisle
1 Brett v2 p173
2 Brett v2 p172
3 HSLC 27/8/1892
4 HSLO 18/8/1894
5 HSLO 28/10/1899
6 HSLO 9/12/1933
7 HSLO 16/4/1938
8 HSLO 14/5/1945
9 HSLO 1/6/1989
10 HSLO 10/7/1992, HRL pub files

Cinque Ports Arms
1 Manwaring-Baines 1986 p362
2 Brett v.2 p155
3 HSLC 15/5/1878
4 HSLO 8/4/1989

Clarence, Middle Street
1 HSLC 2/9/1868
2 HSLC 17/4/1889
3 Tresise 1983 p101
4 HSLO 15/5/1872
5 HSLO 3/2/1894
6 HSLO 28/4/1894
7 HSLO 15/12/1906
8 HSLO 10/11/1906
9 Charles Banks interview 2008

Clarence@Silverhill
1 HSLC 28/1/1874
2 HSLC 3/4/1889
3 HSLO 25/10/1913
4 HSLO 23/5/1914
5 HSLO 13/2/1915
6 HSLO 20/12/1975
7 E-mails to the author 30/10, 5/11/2007

Clifton Tavern
1 HSLC 27/8/1870
2 HSLC 6/2/1895
3 HSLC 6/3/1895
4 HSLO 27/9/1913
5 HSLO 17/2/1923
6 HSLO 6/4/1944
7 HSLO 13/4/1942
8 HSLO 6/10/1945

Clive Vale Hotel
1 HSLC 27/8/1879, 28/8/1883, 23/9/1885, 22/9/1886
2 History Group Newsletter 7. 2008
3 HSLO 15/5/1909
4 HSLO 7/2/1920
5 History Group Hastings Voices p40
6 HSLO 3/12/1987
7 HSLO 8/12/1988

Clown
1 Hastings Directory 1888
2 HSLO 11/2/1905
3 HSLO 22/3/1930
4 HSLO 10/3/1928
5 HSLO 22/3/1930
6 HSLO 16/2/1949
7 HSLO 6/2/1954
8 HSLO 8/12/1956
9 Roger Povey interview 2008

Cricketers
1 HSLC 31/8/1864
2 Ball 1973 p97
3 Tressell 1955 p179

Crown Inn
1 Manwaring-Baines 1986 p362
2 Brett Historico Biographies v3 p178
3 Brett v2 p161
4 Quoted in Manwaring-Baines 1986 p362
5 HSLC 21/6, 26/7, 30/8, 18/10/1854
6 Brett v5 p91

Crown Inn (contd)
7 Brett v6 p58
8 HSLC 4/1/1893
9 HSLO 24/3/1900
10 HSLO 19/3/1921

Cutter
1 Quoted in HSLO 11/9/1971
2 Manwaring-Baines 1986 p362
3 HSLC 1/1/1862
4 HSLC 15/4/1868
5 HSLC 7/2/1872
6 HSLC 4/6/1879
7 HSLC 19/3/1892
8 Peak 1987 p31
9 HSLO 27/1/1995

Dripping Spring
1 Sussex Directory 1866
2 HSLC 28/8/1893
3 HSLO 3/6/1916
4 HSLO 5/2/1938
5 Whitbread inn signs. Series 1 No. 8
6 Cyril Pelluet interview 2008
7 Pat Dunn interview 2009

First In Last Out
1 Hastings Directory 1871
2 Hastings Directory 1880
3 HSLC 28/8/1901
4 HSLO 1/1/1910
5 HSLO 9/3, 20/7, 27/7/1929
6 HSLO 1/11/1930
7 HSLO 18/3/1933
8 HSLO 6/2/1954
9 HSLO 20/11/1982

Foresters Arms
1 Brett v2 p148
2 HSLC 20/8/1856
3 HSLN 3/1/1851
4 HSLC 9/3/1864
5 HSLC 21/10/1874
6 Hastings Directories 1886-90

7 HSLO 4/3/1905
8 HSLO 18/3/1933
9 HSLO 16/2/1952
10 HSLO 20/9/1969

Fortune of War
1 Manwaring-Baines 1986 p362
2 Brett v2 p205
3 HSLN 27/8/1850
4 HSLC 20/5/1885
5 HSLO 14/2/1903
6 HSLO 11/4/1903
7 HSLO 5/10/1968

Fountain
1 HSLN 28/8/1853
2 Coleman 1929 p5
3 HSLC 26/3/1879
4 HSLO 1/7/1916
5 HSLO 13/2/1937
6 Whitbread inn signs. Series 1 No. 4

Fox
1 Sussex Directory 1855
2 HSLC 1/3/1865
3 ROL
4 HSLC 1/9/1897
5 HSLO 21/10/1933
6 HSLO 11/3/1939
7 Alan Crouch interview 2009
8 HSLO 18/5/1940
9 HSLO 11/4/1942
10 Michael Monk interview 2009
11 Pat Dunn interview 2009
12 Whitbread inn signs. Series 1 No. 7

French's Bar
1 HSLN 29/8/1851
2 rootschat.com
3 Sussex directory 1855
4 Brett v6 p211
5 HSLC 1/3/1865
6 HSLC op cit
7 HSLN 2/11/1866, HSLC 26/10/1866

French's Bar (contd)
8 Pat Dunn interview 2009
9 HSLO 13/7/1994

Hare and Hounds
1 Hastings Bygones v6 p31
2 HSLO 30/6/1962
3 HSLO 7/7/1962
4 HSLO 6/2/1909
5 HSLO 22/12/1933, 5/1/1934

Hastings Arms
1 Manwaring-Baines 1986 p363
2 Brett v2 p157
3 Brett v3 p262, p323
4 HSLN 7/2/1851
5 HSLN 25/7/1851
6 HSLO 27/1/1917
7 HSLO 13/3/1926
8 HSLO 29/4/1961
9 HSLO 9/8/1980

Havelock
1 HRL file
2 HSLC 29/7/1874
3 HSLC 25/3/1874
4 HSLC 28/11/1883
5 Goodwin 2005 p84
6 Cyril Pelluet interview 2008
7 HRL file

**Hole in the Wall and
the Kicking Donkey**
1 Manwaring-Baines p363
2 HSLO 13/3/1926
3 HSLO 9/1/1937
4 HSLO 12/3/1938
5 Aspect Southern no.16 1992
6 HSLO 16/2/1952
7 HSLO 14/8/1971
8 Sussex Directory 1855
9 HSLO 15/2/1936
10 HSLO 15/3/1947

Horse and Groom
1 Brett v1 p5
2 Brett op cit p38
3 Brett v2 p125, v3 p262
4 Brett v1 p100
5 Brett v1 p107
6 HSLC 17/10/1860
7 HSLO 24/2, 14/7, 21/7/1917
8 HSLO 17/10/1985
9 HSLO 25/6/1999

Jenny Lind
1 Manwaring-Baines 1986 p363
2 HSLO 19/1/1918
3 HSLO 9/9/1933
4 HSLO 15/2/1941
5 HSLO 17/2/1951
6 HSLO 24/1/1959
7 HSLO 21/8/1982
8 HSLO 7/9/1990

Jolly Fisherman
1 Manwaring-Baines 1986 p363
2 Brett v4 p225
3 HSLC 16/1/1856
4 HSLN 26/1/1855
5 HSLC 3/10/1883
6 Peak 1987 p67
7 HSLO 16/1/1915
8 HSLO 28/3/1925
9 HSLO 14/2/1959

Laila
1 HSLN 24/8/1857
2 HSLC 28/8/1867
3 HSLC 27/8/1890
4 HSLO 23/12/1899
5 Whitbread inn signs. Series 1 No. 5

Lord Nelson
1 Manwaring-Baines 1986 p364
2 Peak 1987 p 43
3 HSLN 27/10/1882
4 HSLO 11/2/1905

Lord Nelson (contd)
5 HSLO 18/2, 4/3, 27/5/1911
6 HSLO 19/3/1938
7 HSLO 11/3/1967
8 Peter Skinner interview 2008
9 Mick Nurse interview 2009
10 HSLO 22/5/1982
11 HSLO 3/8/1989

Marina Fountain
1 Manwaring-Baines 1986 p362
2 Prothero v6 p567
3 Ibid.
4 1851 Census
5 Brett v4 p12
6 HSLG 28/1/1860
7 Brett v4 p105
8 HSLN 3/9/1864
9 HSLO 14/7/1917
10 HSLO 20/4/1968
11 Trefor Holloway interview 2009

Moda
1 Sussex Directory 1866
2 HSLN 24/8/1866
3 urbandictionary.com
4 HSLC 14/9/1870
5 HSLC 12/5/1875
6 HSLC 12/10/1887
7 Charles Banks interview 2008
8 HSLO 1/12/1945
9 Longmate 1975 p216
10 Peter Skinner interview 2008

Nag's Head
1 HSLN 28/8/1853
2 HSLN 24/8/1855
3 HSLC 10/9/1862, 29/10/1862
4 HSLC 31/5/1876
5 HSLC 29/8/1877
6 HSLC 25/11/1885, HSLC 7/11/1888
7 Ball 1973 p97
8 Whitbread inn signs. Series 5 No. 28
9 Michael Rose interview 2009
10 HSLO 3/2/1968

Norman Arms
1 Cousins 1920 p271.
2 Brett v4 p155
3 HSLC 8/4/1868
4 HSLO 4/3/1905
5 HSLO 3/8/1957
6 HSLO 15/3/1920
7 HSLO 20/5/1939
8 HSLO 7/3/1985

North Star
1 HSLO 28/8/1870
2 HSLC 10/1/1877
3 HSLC11/9/1878
4 HSLC 4/9/1878
5 HSLC 12/11/1884, HSLC 12/11/1890
6 HSLC 20/5/1891
7 HSLO 25/3/1939, HSLO 6/1/1940

Old England
1 Quoted in HSLO 23/3/1905
2 Manwaring-Baines 1986 p363
3 Ibid.
4 HSLO 6/1/1940
5 HSLC 25/9/1872
6 HSLC 20/3/1867
7 HSLO 28/7/1894
8 HSLO 9/7/1910

Old King John
1 HSLC 7/9/1870
2 HSLC 27/8/1879
3 HSLN 28/8/1878
4 HSLC 15/10/1892
5 Hastings Voices 2002 p39
6 HSLO 23/11/1940
7 Alan Crouch interview 2009
8 HSLO 6/12/1984

Pig in Paradise
1 HSLC 2/1/1889
2 HSLO 28/4/1894
3 HSLC 30/9/1891
4 HSLO 19/6/1909

Pig in Paradise (contd)
5 HSLO 10/3/1917
6 HSLO 31/7/1926, 21/8/1926
7 HSLO 14/4/1928
8 Pat Dunn interview 2009
9 Alan Crouch interview 2009
10 Cyril Pelluet interview 2008
11 HSLO 13/3/1986

Pissarro's
1 HSLC 31/8/1864
2 Whitbread inn signs. Series 1 No. 3
3 Mick Nurse interview 2009
4 Alan & Marie Garaty interview 2009
5 HSLO 22/4/1994
6 pissarros.co.uk
7 hastingsbeatlesday.org.uk
8 Sergio Guerreiro interview 2008

Prince Albert
1 Manwaring-Baines 1986 p362
2 HSLO 15/3/1913
3 Dyer & Vint 1972 p12
4 Dyer & Vint 1972 p10
5 HSLO 9/1/1937, 15/1/1938
6 Dyer & Vint 1972 p44
7 Ibid.
8 HSLO 17/6/1967

Prince of Wales
1 Sussex Directory 1855
2 HSLC 21/4/1858
3 HSLC 27/8/1862
4 HSLC 23/2/1859
5 HSLC 13/7/1864
6 HSLC 11/12/1867
7 HSLC 12/6/1878
8 HSLO 12/2/1949
9 Pat Dunn interview 2009

Priory
1 HSLC 31/8/1864
2 HSLC 24/5/1865
3 HSLC 17/6/1891

4 HSLO 26/8/1899
5 HSLO 26/8/1916
6 Roger Povey interview 2008

Queen Adelaide
1 HSLC 19/9/1855
2 HSLC 12/5/1857
3 HSLC 27/5/1863
4 HSLN 28/8/1870
5 HSLO 2/10/1872
6 HSLC 2/1/1884
7 HSLO 16/1/1915
8 HSLO 24/10/1936

Railway and the Royal
1 HSLC 27/8/1862
2 HSLC 30/8/1876, 20/9/1876
3 HSLC10/10/1877
4 Hastings Directory 1884
5 HSLC 16/9/1891
6 HSLO 10/2/1917
7 HSLO 8/11/1919
8 Pat Dunn interview 2009
9 Cyril Pelluet interview 2008

Red House
1 ROL
2 HSLC 18/10/1893
3 HSLO 6/1/1894
4 HSLO 15/3/1913
5 HSLO 27/1/1917
6 HSLO 17/3/1951

Roebuck
1 HSLO 16/9/1961
2 HSLC 25/10/1854
3 HSLC 29/8/1860
4 HSLC 25/11/1885, 28/11/1888
5 HSLC 28/8/1895
6 HSLC 28/8/1917
7 HSLC 13/4/1918

Royal Albion
1 HSLO 6/12/1968
2 Brett v4 p194
3 HSLC 27/6/1855, HSLC 2/11/1865
4 HSLC 11/12/1867
5 HSLC 10/1/1877
6 HSLC 27/8/1879
7 HSLO 29/9/1894
8 HSLO 21/8/1915
9 HSLO 13/7/1963
10 Alan Crouch interview 2009

Royal Standard
1 HSLN 29/8/1856
2 HSLC 12/10/1887, 4/4/1888
3 HSLO 15/3/1913
4 HSLO Ibid.
5 HSLO 16/1/1915
6 HSLO 1/7/1967
7 HSLO 2007

Smugglers
1 Sussex Directory 1845
2 Brett v4 p50
3 Brett v4 p224
4 HSLC 23/9/1868
5 HSLC 11/11/1891
6 HSLC 27/10/1894
7 HSLO 3/5/1916
8 HSLO 2/2/1946
9 HSLO 9/11/1946
10 HSLO 8/3/1947
11 Dunkling & Wright 1987 p287
12 Prothero v7 p761

Stag
1 Manwaring-Baines 1986 p366
2 HSLO 6/11/1982
3 HSLO 1/9/1995

Street
1 HSLC 2/9/1868
2 HSLC 4/3/1891
3 HSLC 27/8/1893

4 HSLO 29/9/1894
5 Taylor 2009
6 HSLO 12/9/1936
7 HSLO 26/2/1944
8 Peter Skinner interview 2008
9 HSLO 6/2/1971

Swan
1 Manwaring-Baines 1986 p266
2 HSLC 1/11/1854
3 *Oxford English Dictionary* 1989
4 Parliamentary Papers 1852
5 PHS Journal 2009, HSLC 30/8/1865
6 HSLC 28/8/1889
7 HSLC 9/5/1888
8 HSLC 7/3/1888.
9 HSLO 13/2/1932, 12/3/1932
10 Goodwin 2005 p81
11 HSLO 3/7/1943
12 HSLO 29/6/1946

Tubman and the Dripping Well
1 Sussex Directory 1845
2 Hastings Directory 1884
3 Jim Davidson interview 2008
4 HSLO 24/2/1900
5 HSLO 13/2/1937
6 HSLO 17/2/1934
7 Goodwin 2005 p34
8 Jim Davidson interview 2008
9 Peter Skinner interview 2008
10 HSLO 5/2/1983

Warrior's Gate
1 Brett. v1. p86
2 Brett v3 p277, p308, HSLC 7/6/1854
3 HSLG 11/2/1860
4 Goodwin 2005 p80
5 HSLO 28/5/1943, 3/7/1943
6 HSLO 26/02/1977
7 Pat Dunn interview 2009
8 HSLO 27/3/1976
9 Prothero v4 p393
10 Whitbread inn signs. Series 1 No. 6

Wheatsheaf and the Bricklayer's Arms
1 Research into the Jinks family.
  Cyril Pelluet, 2009 (unpublished).
2 Brett v1 p107
3 HSLO 18/1/1873
4 HSLO 10/2/1917
5 HSLO 23/8/1919
6 HSLN 17/11/1865
7 HSLC 30/5/1866
8 Cyril Pelluet interview 2008

Wishing Tree and the Hollington Oak
1 HSLO 29/6/1946
2 Whitbread inn signs Series 1 No 2
3 Dadson 1994 p5
4 Bullock 1949 p 291
5 Anon *Tales from around the Wishing Tree*. nd. p67
6 ROL
7 Bullock 1949 p282
8 Dadson 1994 p6
9 Prothero v8 p1094
10 HSLO 1/7/1972
11 HSLO 2/4/1993

Ye Olde Pumphouse
1 HRL file
2 Prothero v1 p256
3 Cyril Pelluet interview 2008
4 Michael Rose interview 2009
5 Peter Skinner interview 2008
6 HSLO 6/3/1926

York Hotel
1 HSLN 27/8/1852
2 HSLN 26/8/1853
3 HSLG 12/5/1860
4 HSLC 9/2/1876
5 HSLC 27/8/1879
6 HSLO 22/8/1896
7 HSLO 28/8/1897
8 HSLO 3/7/1915
9 HSLO 10/3/1917, 7/4/1917
10 Charles Banks interview 2008
11 Alan Crouch interview 2009
12 HSLO 8/2/1964

List of Sources

Hastings Directories: 1852–1974 Hastings Reference Library

Sussex Directories: 1828–1866 Brighton History Centre

Census Returns: 1841–1891

Register of Licensees: 1810–1960 (incomplete copy with the author).

Parliamentary Papers: Select Committee on Public Houses 1852–1853.

Books:
Anon (2000) *Tales from around the Wishing Tree*. University of Sussex: Centre for Continuing Education.
Ball, F.C., (1973) *One of the Damned*. London: Lawrence & Wishart.
Bullock, F.W.B., (1949) *A History of the "Church in the Wood" Hollington, Sussex*. St. Leonards-on-Sea: Budd & Gillatt.
Coleman, G.D., (1929) *Queen's Road in 1929*. Hastings Reference Library.
Cousins, H., (1920) *Hastings of Bygone Days and the Present*. Hastings: F.J. Parsons
Dadson, R.E., (1994) *History of the Wishing Tree Public House*. Photocopy, Hastings Reference Library.
Dictionary of National Biography. Volume 25. (2004) Oxford University Press.
Dunkling, L. and Wright, G., (1987) *A Dictionary of Pub Names*. London: Routledge & Kegan Paul.
Dyer, W.H. and Vint, A.K., (1972) *Winkle Up! The Story of the Hastings Winkle Club*. Hastings Winkle Club.
Funnell, B., (1999) *The America Ground*. Hastings Area Archaeological Research Group.
Goodwin, N.D., (2005) *Hastings at War*. Chichester: Phillimore.
Harrison, B., (1971) *Drink and the Victorians: Temperance Question in England, 1815–1872*. Keel University Press.
Hyde, A., (2004) *The Breeds of Hastings: Merchants and Brewers. 1762–1931*. Brewery History Society.
Jennings, P., (2007) *The Local: A History of the English Pub*. Stroud: Tempus.
Longmate, N., (1975) *The GIs: The Americans in Britain 1942–1945*. London: Hutchinson.
Manwaring-Baines, J., (1986) *Historic Hastings*. St. Leonards-on-Sea: Cinque Port Press Ltd.
Mass Observation (1945) *The Pub and the People*. London: Ebury Press.
Matthews, M., (2003) *Alf Cobb. Mugsborough Rebel: The Struggle for Justice in Edwardian Hastings*. St Leonards-on-Sea: Hastings Press.

Oxford English Dictionary 1989 Oxford University Press.
Peak, S., (1987) *Fishermen of Hastings*. Hastings: SpeaksBooks.
Taylor, A.R., (2009) *Played at the Pub: The Pub Games of Britain*. English Heritage.
Tresise, C.E., (1983) *Tavern Treasures: A Book of Pub Collectables*. Poole: Blandford Press.
Tressell, R., (1965) *The Ragged Trousered Philanthropists*. London: Grafton Books.

Volumes: -
Brett, T.B., *Manuscript History*. Volumes 1–7. Hastings Reference Library.
Brett, T.B., *Hastings Historico Biographies*. Hastings Reference Library.
Hastings Local History Group. (2002) *A History of Ore*.
Hastings Local History Group. (2002) *Hastings Voices*.
Hastings Local History Group. (1998–2007) *Hastings Bygones, Volumes 1–6*.
Hastings Modern History Workshop. (1984) *Central Hastings, The Early Years*.
Hastings Modern History Workshop. (1997) *Priory Meadow and the Town Centre*.
Prothero, J., Scrapbooks, *Volumes 1–9*. Hastings Reference Library.

Newspapers and Periodicals: -
Aspect Southern No.16. (1992) Hastings Reference Library file World War II.
Cinque Ports Chronicle: 1838–1841
Hastings and St Leonards Chronicle: 1846–1905
Hastings and St Leonards Gazette: 1856–1896
Hastings and St Leonards News: 1848–1876
Hastings and St Leonards Observer: 1866–2000
Hastings Pictorial Advertiser: 1901–1918

Websites: -
hastingsbeatlesday.org.uk
hastingsjack.co.uk
pissarros.co.uk
rootschat.com
thecopperfamily.com
urbandictionary.com

Oral history: -
The late Charles Banks, Alan Crouch, Jim Davidson, Pat Dunn, Alan Garaty, Marie Garaty, Sergio Guerreiro, John Hodges, Trefor Holloway, Trevor Hopper, Michael Monk, Mick Nurse, Cyril Pelluet, Roger Povey, Michael Rose, Peter Skinner.

Genealogical research: -
Jinks family (2008–9) Cyril Pelluet (unpublished).

APPENDIX 1

Pub–Population Ratio
Hastings 1824–1941

year	public houses	beer houses	total	population	pub–population ratio		
1824	15	5	20	4,000			1/200
1836	34	____	34	6,000			1/176
1850	43	33	76	9,500			1/112
1860	70	55	125	14,000			1/110
1864	79	60	139	20,000			1/143
1870	99	*52	151	26,000			1/172
1897	128	52	180	*58,000			1/322
1906	137	37	174	*59,000			1/339
1928	_____			63,000		Eastbourne Blackpool	1/331 1/574 1/711
1937	_____			65,000			1/331
1941	121	17	138	66,000			1/478

* estimated

sources: brewster sessions, directories, www.visionofbritain.org.uk

APPENDIX 2

The lost pubs of Hastings and St Leonards

This list of 178 lost pubs and beer houses, is not exhaustive or comprehensive and there are many others. However, it does indicate the turnover of public houses in Hastings and St Leonards over the last two centuries. Those listed in italics have their history in the main text. Information about any of them would be welcomed by the author.

Admiral Benbow, London Road
Albert Hotel, Queens Road
Albert Shades, Undercliffe
Alma
Anchor, East Ascent.
Ancient Druids, George Street
Baker's Arms, Halton
Bedford Arms, Queen's Road
Bee Hive, Wellington Court
Bell, High Street
Belle Vue, Marine Parade
Bird in Hand, South Street
Black Horse, Priory Road, Halton
Black Spread Eagle, Courthouse Street
Bohemia Arms, Bohemia Road
Bowra's BH, Pelham Street
Bricklayer's Arms, Bohemia
Bricklayer's Arms, Warrior Square
Britannia, Bourne Street
British Hotel, Mercatoria
Burfield's BH, White Rock Street
Canteen, Halton
Carpenter's Arms, Priory Road
Castle Shades, Castle Street
Catt BH, 46½ All Saints Street
Clifton, Stainsby Street
Clive Vale Hotel, Alfred Road
Coach and Horses, Mews Road
Coleman BH, Commercial Road

Cottage, Hughenden Place
Cottage Inn, St Andrew's Road
Cottage of Content, London Road
Cricketers, South Terrace
Crouch BH, Castle Terrace
Crown and Three Mackerel
Cruttenden's BH
Crystal Palace
Cutter Foam, Tackle Way
Dawkin's BH, Norman Road East
Denmark Arms, Denmark Place
Derby Arms, Alfred Street
Diamond Inn, Bourne Walk
Dorset Arms, Duke Road
Duke of Cornwall, Post Office Passage
Duke of Cumberland, Stonebeach
Duke of York, Alfred Street
Dun Horse, Albion Street, Halton
Druids Inn, George Street
Drum
Eagle Tavern, Bourne Street
Earl of Arundel, Havelock Road
Edinburgh Castle, St Georges Road
Eight Bells, Courthouse Street
Eversfield Arms
Fishermen's Home, East Hill Passage
Foresters Arms, Sheppard Street
Foresters Tavern, Pinder Road
Fortune of War, Priory Road

Freemason's Tavern, Wellington Place
Free Trader, Fishmarket
Gaiety, Queen's Road.
George, George Street
George Inn, All Saint's Street
Globe, Meadow Road
Granville, St Georges Road (?)
Halton Tavern
Harbour Bar, All Saints Street
Hare and Hounds, Old London Road
Hastings Castle, Wellington Terrace
Hearts of Oak, Bohemia Road
Hole in the Wall, Claremont
Hole in the Wall, Hill Street
Hope BH, East Parade
Hope, Lennox Street, Halton
Hope, West Street
Hope of Freedom, All Saints Street
Hundreds Inn, The Ridge
Johnson's BH, Priory Road
Jolly Fisherman, East Parade
Kentish Arms. East Street
Kicking Donkey, Hill Street
Kings Head, All Saints Street
Kite's Nest
Little Brown Jug, St Mary's Terrace
Lugger, West Street
Mackerel
Maidenhead, High Street
Malvern, Malvern Way
Manor Shades, St Mary's Road
Market Tap, George Street
Market Tavern
Market Tower
Marina, Caves Road
Mason's Arms, High Street
Merry Christmas
Milkman's Arms, Mount Pleasant
Mitre, High Street
New Found Out. Breeds Yard
New Golden Cross, Havelock Road
New Inn, Alfred Street
New Inn. All Saints Street
New Inn, Mercatoria

New Moon, All Saint's Street
New Ship, West Street
Oddfellows, Caves Road
Old House at Home
Old Sam's
Original Good Woman, Fishmarket
Palmerston, Queen's Road
Partridge's BH, Fish Market
Pelican, Fishmarket
Perrin's BH
Pilot, Stone Street
Piper's BH, Commercial Road
Plasterer's Arms, South Street
Pork Farrol's BH, Priory Bridge
Priory, Station Road
Prince Albert, North Street
Prince Albert, Rock a'Nore
Prince of Wales, Bohemia
Prince of Wales, Old Town
Prince of Wales, Pelham Street
Privateer
Provincial Hotel, Havelock Street
Queen Adelaide, West Street
Queen's Head, East Beach Street
Queen's Shades, Harold Place
Railway, Priory Street
Railway Arms BH, Halton
Railway Stores, Hughenden Road
Red Hart, George Street
Red House, Emmanuel Road.
Red Lion, Stone Street
Rising Sun, East Parade
Robin Hood, North Street
Rodrick Inn, High Street
Roebuck, High Street
Roger's BH, George Street
Rose and Crown, George Street
Royal Albion Shades, George Street
Royal Oak, Castle Street
Royal Oak, Oak Passage, High Street
Royal Sussex Arms, Old London Road
Saunders BH, Mews Road
Ship, Bourne Street
Shipwright's Arms, Castle Street

Star, High Street
Star in the East, Rock a' Nore Road
Star in the West, Undercliffe
St George's Tavern, St Georges Road
St Leonards Arms, London Rd
St Leonards Tap, Marina
St Michael's Tavern
Sun Inn, Tackleway
Sussex Tap, Marina
Swan, High Street
Swan Shades, Hill Street
Three Partridges
Tiger, Stonefield Road
Two Sawyers
Tyrell's BH, All Saint's Street
Victoria Tavern, High Street

Volunteer Inn, Middle Street
Warrior's Arms, Norman Road
Warrior's Gate, London Road
Watermen's Arms
Webb's BH, East Street
Wheeler's BH, East Beach Street
White's BH, Bourne Street
White Friars, Priory Road
White Hart, Norman Road
White Harte, St Clements
White Horse, Silverhill
White Lion, Dorset Place
White Lion, St Michael's Terrace
Windsor's BH, Tivoli
Wood's BH, West Street
York Hotel, Wellington Place

The Hole in the Wall and the Kicking Donkey